The Artist
and the Orchard

A Memoir

The Artist
and the Orchard

A Memoir

Linda Hoffman

LP

Loom Press
Amesbury, Massachusetts
2021

The Artist and the Orchard: A Memoir
Copyright © 2021 by Linda Hoffman
lindahoffman.com
All rights reserved
Printed in the United States of America
First Edition

ISBN: 978-0-931507-22-9

Book design by Lynn Horsky
Cover painting by Linda Hoffman
Photographs on page 185 and back cover by Kelly Fitzsimmons
Photograph on page *ix* by Robert Hesse
Versa Press, Inc., Peoria, Illinois

Loom Press
15 Atlantic View, Amesbury, Massachusetts 01913
www.loompress.com
info@loompress.com

All events are true, however the passage of time has been compressed
to create a narrative flow. Several names have been changed to protect
the privacy of certain persons.

The section quotations are from *The Apple Tree* by Liberty Hyde Bailey
published in 1922. While approaches to growing fruit have greatly
changed since his time, Bailey offers keen observations and deep
respect for the apple tree and all its creatures.

For Alex, Nick, and Ariel

A place belongs forever to whoever claims it hardest, remembers it most obsessively, wrenches it from itself, shapes it, renders it, loves it so radically that he remakes it in his image . . . .

—Joan Didion, *The White Album*

Contents

Where Are the Apples?

The apple-tree starts life fresh and vigorous. It grows rapidly. The shoots are long and straight. The wood is smooth and fair and supple . . . . But in time the difficulties come. The tree probably slows down. It becomes too thick of branches. The land is not tilled. It is not manured. Insects and fungi make headway . . . . The tree becomes broken diseased, gnarly, unshapely.

—Liberty Hyde Bailey

Row 1: It's Hard to Grow Apples

I was alone in an abandoned orchard and didn't know the first thing about growing apples.

Holding a half-sheet of paper, I read the names of varieties by row— McIntosh, Cortland, Red Delicious, Blushing Golden, and Golden Delicious. A few small green orbs dangled here and there, but I couldn't tell a McIntosh from a Cortland. Thorns on brambles snagged my ankles while poison ivy and bittersweet vines spiraled around tree trunks. This was not what I expected in a New England apple orchard in July. The enormity of my new reality hit me.

On a bright March afternoon in 2001, I'd visited A & M Orchards in Harvard, a rural town in eastern Massachusetts about forty-five minutes west of Boston. The real estate listing said: *Farmhouse with five bedrooms, a detached barn/garage, apple orchard, and chicken coop.* I wasn't looking for a way to get back to the earth or grow my own food. I was leaving a long marriage and looking for a home for myself and my three children. I would never have considered a small farm, but a good friend had urged me to check out the property. She had grown up here and

The farmhouse in 2001

loved this old homestead. Her parents had sold it to the present owners.

I called my friend Roger, a local realtor. He questioned whether the property was a good match, but he said he'd meet me there. I arrived first and ignored the in-need-of-paint clapboard farmhouse. Instead, I walked down the driveway towards the pond and a towering elm tree. All across America these elegant trees had died from Dutch elm disease, and yet, here against the open sky, isolated from other elms, this tree was thriving. Its thin branches swayed, zigzagging their reflections across the surface of the water. The elm had been planted alongside a ten-foot-high stone dam. Water flowed from the large pond into a smaller one below. The sound of falling water reminded me of ancient Chinese Buddhist hermits doing ablutions under cold mountain falls. I was a little nervous visiting this farm property, but the mystery and uniqueness of the landscape stirred my curiosity.

Roger and I entered the house. The front door opened into a spacious living room where a brick fireplace covered one wall. A brown sofa, a dark upholstered chair, and a wooden desk floated like atolls on the hardwood floor. Adrift among them, I followed Roger down three steps into the kitchen where molasses-colored pine boards covered the walls and ceiling. In place of drawers and cabinets, open shelves held plates, bowls, and glasses. Along one wall, heavy pots for making jam and stocks sat on the floor. Above an old-fashioned cast-iron cookstove a patchwork of blackened pans hung, their undersides crusty with use. On my search for a new home, I had already toured several houses whose kitchens boasted granite counters and sleek appliances. This farmhouse kitchen had a different feel—its rustic patina was more my style.

Roger and I continued our tour upstairs and peered into simple bedrooms. My three children would each have a room. The master bedroom windows faced the raspberry patch to the east and wetlands to the south, five hundred acres of conservation land owned by the United States Department of Fish and Wildlife. The master bath had 1960s avocado-colored fixtures, a hue that made me want to look away, but my right hand reached towards the sink's hot water faucet and I thought,

If this house has hot water, it will be fine.

I followed Roger downstairs and out the door.

"Is it all right to walk around the pond?"

"Sure, go ahead. I'll wait on the porch."

He didn't seem to relish a trek through March's mud and patches of old snow.

I followed the contour of the water, over a small stone bridge to the other side. That's when I saw a rock formation the size of a Volkswagen in the middle of the lower pond. It looked like a giant turtle gazing towards the rising sun. A domed boulder formed the body and a smaller stone shaped the head.

My middle child, Nick, loves turtles and for many years kept an Eastern box turtle named Pebble as a pet. Friends and family sent him turtle mementos in ebony, teak, alabaster, jade, cloth, and corn husk from Russia, Guatemala, and Thailand. When he was a young boy, Nick taught me how to make stone turtles outdoors, choosing a large stone for the body, a smaller one for the head, four pebbles for legs, and a narrow one for the tail. We would leave these turtle totems in the landscape on hikes from the tip of Cape Cod to the summit of Mt. Washington in New Hampshire, where we made a harrowing climb up Huntington's Ravine together. I didn't know if the property owners had ever seen this "turtle," but I took it as a good omen.

I rejoined Roger and asked, "Can I see the chicken coop?"

Walking into a ramshackle white clapboard shed, I teased away curtains of cobwebs. Slimy green chicken shit mixed with sawdust covered the floor. Some forty old hens squawked, panicked by my presence. I breathed in the dust scratched up by their overgrown toenails. Later I learned the roosters' endless mounting was the cause of the hens' featherless backs.

"What's going to happen to all these birds?" I asked.

"Why? Do you want them?"

Why not? I thought, not knowing anything about chickens. "Maybe."

"I'll ask the owners," Roger said.

An orange tractor overfilled the other side of the chicken coop. Roger said, "The tractor comes with the property."

I looked away. *What was I going to do with this giant relic of a machine?* My art background hadn't prepared me for driving a tractor.

Near the coop, a rickety fence marked the wintered-over remains of a kitchen garden. I had grown vegetables in small raised beds, but this sizable plot was a feed-a-family-all-year garden.

Next came the detached barn/garage where the owner had stored Model T cars. As a professional sculptor, I needed a space for my studio. The cars were gone, only oil splotches on the wood plank floor remained. A few small windows let in light. My rusty metal objects, tools, and machines would fit. It wouldn't take much to bring in some heat.

"Where are the apples?" The listing had mentioned an orchard. I didn't know what I would do with it, but I wanted to see everything.

We crossed the road and walked down a narrow cart trail. The rows of old trunks and branches stretched out in wavy lines. The ground was bare, Persephone had yet to rise.

"What will you do with the orchard?" Roger asked.

"I don't know."

"It's hard to grow apples. And this orchard needs a lot of care."

We continued walking down the cart road about a quarter of a mile until we reached a small clearing. I peered into a weathered shed. Earth-encrusted tools stood silently in their stalls like pterodactyls. I wondered if they, too, came with the property. Before I could ask, Roger had turned back towards the house.

※

Apples figure in mythology, history, science, and religion, but they appear most significantly in art. Van Gogh painted rows of apple trees in blossom, their repetition of trunks lining the bucolic streets of Arles in southern France. Cezanne painted this humble fruit over and over again, his paintings of apples some of the most memorable work in the history of modern art. He's even quoted as saying, "With an apple, I will astonish Paris." Henri Matisse painted apples throughout his life. In his painting *Still Life with Apples*, 1925, four yellow apples sit on a bunched-up pink tablecloth—the table, like an unmoored boat, floats against a background of blues. These apples seem as if they might roll off the painting. I was aware of this *apple* art history, but it didn't occur to me to wonder if the orchard would make its way into my art.

When I moved to New England in my early twenties, I learned that apple picking is the quintessential fall activity for New Englanders. Having grown up outside of Philadelphia in the industrial city of Chester, Pennsylvania, I had no experience with apple trees. Walking through this tangled orchard, I was intrigued. I planned to visit the farm again.

This time I brought Ariel, my twelve-year-old daughter. We looked at the bedroom upstairs I thought would suit her, and I pointed out she'd have her own bathroom. She asked if she could have a day bed, one of those combinations that is a bed and a sofa at the same time. I said, "Of course!" Sitting on stools at a counter in the kitchen I asked, "Would the house be all right?" She nodded, *Yes.* My boys, Nick, fourteen, and Alex, seventeen, came with me on another visit. Alex wanted the smallest bedroom with the sloped ceiling while Nick took the room with a view of the pond.

When the boys and I walked outside to look around Alex asked, "Do you think there are fish in the pond?" Alex always loved fishing. At six years old, with a small rod and reel, he pulled in a sunfish, unhooked it, and kissed it on the lips before he threw it back.

Nick announced, "There's enough space for a trampoline!" I promised whatever one he chose.

I wanted my children to like the farm. Like tender seedlings, they had a lot to adapt to. Putting my own longing for happiness over keeping the family together left me feeling guilty and selfish. I was excited about the possibilities of the farm, but I also heard a chorus of voices intoning, *You can't do this. Forget it. You don't deserve this.*

I told a friend, "I don't know if I can manage such a large property." She replied, "Just do it."

That little nudge was what I needed. Like a boat tipping over the falls, this rundown farm, A & M Orchards, named for the present owners, Art and Marie Spaulding, would become our new home. ❦

Row 2: Diesel, Dodder, and Raspberries

Before signing papers, Art Spaulding surprised me by suggesting a tractor lesson. *I guess he thinks I'm going to need the tractor.* We made a date, and I met him as he was pulling it out of the chicken coop. "Now you climb up." I hauled myself up and sat on the torn black plastic while he pointed out the stick on the right of the steering wheel to shift gears and the stick on the left to shift from forward to reverse. I scooched to the front edge of the seat because I was too short to reach the clutch and accelerator pedals at the same time.

"Now, shift up," Art instructed.

"No, you have to keep the clutch fully in," he shouted as the engine coughed.

Soon I was able to drive in a circle and shift gears fairly smoothly. I came to a stop.

"Two rules. Always put on the parking brake when you stop, and lower the bucket to the ground. The parking brake is that little wire. Pull it up while you press down on the brake."

"Now, lower the bucket," he said. "See the instructions near the

Roadside signage for Old Frog Pond Farm

bucket controller."

On a faded sticker I saw the words: *float, up, down, down & roll back, down & dump, dump, and up & dump.* There were so many directions. I pushed the stick to the right for down.

"See that lever by your left leg? You don't need it very often, but if you move it backwards you go from two-wheel to four-wheel drive," Art explained. "And there's another lever next to your seat."

I saw the black line drawing of a rabbit and another of a turtle. *The turtle and the hare,* I thought.

"The rabbit puts you in high gear and the turtle in low gear."

I started the engine again and lifted the bucket.

"Release the brake," Art reminded me. "Now shift to turtle gear."

The tractor crept along and I felt the ratcheting down to a singularly slow passage of time. I liked this measured travel. It was peaceful.

Before I left the farm, Art's wife, Marie, handed me two manila folders. One was for the 1985 Kubota tractor and backhoe attachment.

Marie said, "You own only half the backhoe. Ed Baron who lives across the street owns the other half."

The other folder said Chapter 61-A. Marie cautioned me, "You need to fill out Chapter 61-A paperwork every year in order to keep the farm in agricultural use and keep the taxes low. You don't want to forget! If land comes out of 61-A, the new owner must pay all the back taxes owed."

I made a mental note to add time-sensitive reports and important taxes to my new list of responsibilities. My soon-to-be former husband, Paul, had always taken care of this sort of thing.

Marie gave me another paper with the name of Rite Package, a company that sold green pint berry boxes for raspberry picking. It was June, but in a few short months the raspberry crop would be ready to sell. Art and Marie assured me that with eggs and raspberries the farm would easily meet its Chapter 61-A requirement. They made no mention of apples, though, almost as an afterthought, Marie handed me the half-sheet of paper with the list of varieties by row.

As I listened to Marie, the responsibility of the farm grew in my mind to epic proportions. What had I signed up for? I had some financial support from Paul, but I was clearly going to have to embrace the farm emotionally, physically, and spiritually. Buying a house was one thing, but I had signed up for much more. And gnawing like squirrels in the attic was the question, *Can you do this?*

On move-in day, the children were away on Cape Cod for our family's annual summer vacation. I envisioned them gathering without me—Paul, our three children, his four older children, their partners and babies. Being left out of the festivities unnerved me, but I had to begin this new life. And I had to begin it alone.

A few days later, I backed the tractor out of the shed and bumped along the dirt driveway. Diesel smoke spewed from its crooked pipe, and the engine clanged as I shifted gears. The world progressed differently from this new vantage point, and I engaged it in a new way. Then I noticed the gas gauge showed less than a quarter of a tank. Art hadn't mentioned fuel. I parked, remembering to lower the bucket, and went to look for a gas container in the coop. Nothing there. I went off to buy a plastic container and find fuel. The man at the hardware store assured me I should buy a yellow one, for diesel. I'd never filled anything but my car's tank. The warning stickers on the gas pump said *Danger* and *Flammable*. My container felt flimsy. *Will it explode?*

Back home, I found the fuel cap on top of the tractor's radiator. I needed to lift the forty-pound container up and over the tractor's engine. Like a seal ascending a staircase, I climbed up onto the tractor's front tire, grabbed the radiator cover with one hand while opening the gas cap with the other, all the while balancing the fuel container on the tire next to my foot. Then I lifted the much-too-heavy container, poked the spout into the tank, and tried to hold everything steady while squeezing the release trigger. *Do they really expect you to do all this at once?* I hadn't thought of a funnel until it was too late, but I marveled at the fuel's translucent colors as some spilled over the orange tractor body.

A small decal on the side of the tractor said to change the oil, check the brake fluid, and grease the fittings after twenty hours of use. *Grease the fittings.* I knew nothing about these things. To make sculpture I worked with cloth, wood, and metal objects. I used hand tools like drills and electric grinders. I was over my head. I needed some help with the tractor as well as with fence repairs around the vegetable garden. I placed an ad in the local newspaper for some part-time help, and one person responded.

Caleb had left an office job, thankful to be finished with a long commute. He told me he rented an apartment at a farm in the next town. His landlady was an older woman, and he worked as her property manager. He was looking for a few additional hours of work outdoors. He felt sure he could help out at my place in addition to his existing duties. Most important, he was familiar with farm equipment.

On his first day of work, I gave him a tour, including the tools in the shed behind the orchard. Afterwards he said, "Linda, I should hook up the brush hog and mow the orchard."

"What?" I asked, picturing some large bovine contraption.

"You have one out back in the implement shed. It's a mower that will cut through heavy brush."

Now I remembered the prehistoric creatures in the implement shed.

Caleb mowed the orchard, and then told me he thought the grass was getting too long.

"Yes, it is," I replied. I assumed he would use the brush hog.

"I can't mow the grass with the brush hog. Is there a lawnmower?"

My mind flash-toured the farm—in the coop, under my studio, in the implement shed. I went lawnmower shopping the next day.

Over that first summer, I focused on the raspberry patch on the far side of the house. The farm had a third of an acre of fall berries, and the canes were already waist high. The Spauldings had explained they missed the window for putting down a pre-emergent herbicide, something they said I must do every year in early spring. It didn't matter. It didn't sound like anything I wanted to use. I simply set to work weeding with a hand trowel and pitchfork. But there was "dodder."

The Spauldings had cautioned me about the dodder vine and rightly so. An invasive plant from Asia with no predators, it cannibalizes trees, fields, even acres of forest. Once the vine makes contact with a plant, it twirls around the host, climbing and suctioning the hosts' stems to draw out nutrients. Photographs of the plant show acres of scraggly forest covered with cobwebs of dodder. In the Midwest, dodder makes whole fields look like Miss Havisham's room in Dickens' *Great Expectations*, neglected and dysfunctional.

I found caches of this parasitic vine throughout the patch. Once you know what to look for, you can't miss its lemon-yellow sinuous threads circling up and around the raspberry canes. Caleb helped me dig out large areas of infected plants. It was that or give up the crop. The dodder was taking over. We bagged the cut canes in large black trash bags that I took to the landfill. Caleb pushed me to be thorough, to clear all the boundaries around the infected plants, while I wanted to remove the smallest number of canes necessary. I hated to pull out so many living plants, so many raspberries.

"Linda," Caleb said. "I think you should put down black plastic to cover the soil where we removed the dodder."

"Black plastic? Can't we just use some mulch?"

"No, you want to be sure no seeds germinate. I think you should leave the plastic down for a couple of years."

Ugly black plastic weaving through the canes was not my aesthetic, but I followed his advice. The dodder was not going to glom onto me. Friends told me I was crazy to have moved here. "What about your art?" they asked. *Yes, I will continue to be an artist. And yes, I have a lot of new responsibilities. And no, I don't have time for anything else.* I didn't know what else to say. I didn't know myself what was propelling me into this new life or whether I would sink or swim. Working hard during the day I was absorbed by the physical labor, but then later I would fall into a mantra of worrisome thoughts. Had I made a mistake? After all, I could have gone in any direction with my hard-won freedom. But I had made a choice. Was it a good one?

Miraculously, the rest of the plants grew and grew. By the end of August the canes were up to my shoulders and the flower clusters had already begun to attract pollinators. The hard green berries transformed into soft red fruit. In sunlight, their crimson sweetness glistened.

Ariel was home and I shouted upstairs, "Come outside with me. We have ripe raspberries!"

Together we picked those first magical fruits. A week later the patch had more berries than we could possibly eat ourselves. Darcy, a neighbor, sent out an email to let the locals know we were in business. At nearby intersections I put out hand-painted signs saying, "Pick Your Own Raspberries" with arrows directing people to the farm. Sure enough, pickers came—mothers pushing strollers, neighbors on their way home from work, and others who had once picked fruit at the farm. The bounty of the berries was astonishing. Standing in one place you could fill a pint within minutes. A couple with broad smiles walked up to me.

"We've been coming here for years to pick raspberries with our two daughters," the man said. "We're so glad the patch is open. I'm Jim, and this is my wife, Susan."

His wife added, "We love these berries—they are the sweetest."

A picker in a flowered skirt asked nervously, "What about those bees?" Honeybees, skinny-waisted wasps, fuzzy bumblebees, unidentified insects of all shapes and sizes buzzed the raspberry rows. She was worried about getting stung.

"See all those chambers in each raspberry—they each have to be pollinated." I had been reading up about raspberries. "But I don't worry about getting stung. The pollinators are so intent on gathering nectar they won't bother you. I don't worry, and I'm allergic to bees."

"What's that?" she gasped pointing to a pitch-black insect with cerulean blue swatches on its sides.

"A mud dauber," I replied.

When the female is about to lay her eggs, she digs a hole in the ground. She then uses her long stinger to kill other insects, usually spiders or katydids, and drags the dead bugs into the hole. She lays one egg on top of them, then goes off and kills two more insects to lay over her egg. When the larva is born, food is waiting. Once the larva grows wings and can fly, it too, will feed on flower nectar.

In the evening, I ritually handpicked Japanese beetles off the raspberry leaves and dropped them into a cup of soapy water. Left on the plants, they devour the leaves and eat the fruit. The Spauldings had suggested putting up scented bags to attract and catch them, but I decided these would only attract more beetles. I soon became quite adept at nabbing the little scarabs before they flew away, able to snatch five or six of them at a time. Ariel sometimes came out and helped, and we'd walk along opposite sides of the row, each carrying a small jar of water to drown the picked-off beetles.

Then we received the news along with the rest of the country. It was 9/11. I walked around the farm in a daze of confusion and powerlessness. The two planes that had left Boston's Logan Airport carried many people from Massachusetts. The Hanson family was from Groton where I had lived, and a teacher in Harvard, my new town, lost her husband. Sophie, my stepdaughter, was alone in New York city with her five-year-old daughter, Gaia. They would leave and come up to Massachusetts to recover from the shock of the loss and feeling of vulnerability.

Our first raspberry season ended with a hard frost on October 8. Marie had told me the berries would continue to ripen until the end of October, but freezing temperatures made the sweetness disappear. Even with the cooler temperatures, the hens were still laying. I took down the Pick-Your-Own Raspberries sign in front of the farm and put up a new one.

Fresh Eggs
from
Cool Chicks

I now had more time to be in the studio, but I couldn't get myself to focus. The haul of old tools and metal I had dragged along with me from my old life seemed to me to be just that—a heap of useless clanging things. I didn't know if I would ever use them again to make sculpture.

I still hadn't done anything about the orchard across the street. The swamp maples glowed red, the heart-shaped catalpa leaves gold, the elm and oak leaves were buttery yellow, but the apple trees gave off a sullen feeling, their leaves wrinkled and brown. Holding onto Marie's list of apple varieties, I walked up and down the rows. Only insect-riddled apples hung here and there. I didn't know where to begin. The map was useless. I shoved it into my back pocket and never saw it again. ✻

Row 3: A Voice of Sanity

In the spring of 2002, the dead trees in the orchard stood out. I could see the difference between the dry and lifeless bark and the patina of life on the branches of the growing trees. Removing all diseased and dead wood from the orchard was my first thought. I tagged the dead trees, and Caleb brought over his chainsaw and began cutting them down, leaving a few feet of trunk sticking out of the ground. Then he used the tractor and a chain to pull out the root systems. I couldn't have done this without him. The root masses were heavy and unwieldy. Boulders remained lodged between the largest roots and soil clung like starfish to rock. For days the orchard buzzed with the razz of the chain saw. I couldn't wait until Caleb stopped.

We set aside the trunks and largest branches for the wood stoves, and carted the prunings and roots to the field on the far side of my studio making five towering pyres. The piles burned for three days. The crackling intense heat brought new energy to the farm. A phoenix rising from the ashes. I was fascinated by the patterns in the charred wood. Each blackened little section aligned with the next one as if part

Beyond the Unknown, sculpture, 2002

of a three-dimensional jigsaw puzzle. It was no longer wood, but had been transformed into some other element. I pulled aside a few pieces to use in sculptures. It was not something the human hand could ever replicate.

Caleb and I backfilled the holes in the orchard where the roots had been wrenched out. I did some pruning of the apple trees following suggestions from the father of one of Ariel's friends. Caleb brush-hogged again between the rows of trees to keep the bittersweet, honeysuckle, and brambles at bay. Together we weeded around each tree pulling out weed after wild weed. It was exhausting, but like in the raspberry patch, I had no thought of spraying an herbicide.

I invited two couples for dinner. One of the men asked, "Linda, what are you doing?"

I didn't know how to answer. .

"I'm farming, and making sculpture, and taking care of my kids."

I heard my answer, but the words felt incomplete. On the surface they were true, but they also weren't true. While I was searching for words to try to explain that this new life had become my quest, my search for the Holy Grail, my friend responded for me, "It's so much work. I don't know how you're going to manage it."

In mid-May, when the local orchards were in bloom, ours produced only a scattering of blossoms. The orchard was suffering. Friends said, "Oh, the orchard must be beautiful." I shook my head.

Caleb said, "Linda, I think you need bees. All the other orchards bring in hives to pollinate the trees when the blossoms are open."

"Caleb, I'm allergic to bees."

"I still think you need some hives. You know I once kept bees. I might still have some equipment."

"Maybe you're right," I sighed, feeling another challenge looming. Bees. How am I going to raise bees?

I still clung to the idea we would bring the orchard back to health. I wouldn't give up. Yes, pollination is obviously crucial. I would do something about pollination.

Meanwhile, I started studying apple care. Apples attract a lot of pests—so many, in fact, reciting them felt like the Kaddish, the Hebrew prayer of mourning. Codling moth, apple maggot fly, plum curculio, leaf roller, sawfly, aphid, the list numbered over 300 pests in New England alone. Apples fall prey to fungal diseases, too: scab, cedar apple rust, black rot, brown rot, powdery mildew, frog-eye leaf spot, as well as a dreaded bacterial woe, fire blight, that can kill an entire tree in one season. The Spauldings hadn't sprayed in five years; health issues had forced them to abandon orchard care. An orchard where the trees have grown dependent on chemical fertilizers and insecticides doesn't do well on its own. Unlike wild apple trees, they are more like hothouse flowers—they haven't developed natural immunities to diseases and pests.

The books I consulted presented the orchard as a battlefield. The solo orchardist is lined up against an army of insects. These books assured me that I was going to need to spray pesticides and, to do that, I would need to get a pesticide license. I found the prospect terrifying. I thought if I could only find someone to help me get started, someone who would do the spraying, I could do the rest, whatever "the rest" was. But this "someone" didn't exist.

Finally, I found a voice of sanity in the book *Your Apple Orchard* by A. P. Thomson, published in 1982.

> With the development of chemically synthesized pesticides, man had a shotgun that he could use to destroy virtually all pests in one blast. But these pesticides began to migrate into his food chain and destroyed much of the natural balances, hence creating even more severe problems affecting the very basis for his own life. Pests became immune to the poisons and new ones developed. We are now at that point where the health of people is on a collision course with catastrophe.

I agreed with him. I couldn't imagine spraying a pesticide toxic to the creatures living in the wetlands surrounding the orchard. I couldn't imagine going to classes so I could get certified to handle toxic chemicals. And I couldn't imagine asking Caleb to do that either. Yet when I searched for a set of specific instructions on how to grow apples naturally, it didn't seem to exist.

I heard myself say, "Caleb, we're going to bring this orchard back, and we're going to do it organically."

I started mentioning to people I was thinking of growing our apples organically, even though I had no idea what this decision entailed. The reply I received was always the same: "Oh, that's really hard."

I simply stopped listening to the naysayers. The degree of difficulty did not change the facts. I wanted to bring back the orchard, and I wanted to do it organically. I now had a vision I could hang onto. Maybe I was engaging in some magical thinking, but I was going to try. Even though I hadn't tasted one apple, I was determined to make it work.

I needed to contact someone who grew apples locally. Calls to two of the neighboring orchards were discouraging. Each time, the person who answered the phone had no interest in speaking with me. Of course, they were busy with their own orchards, and I was a nuisance. Harvard is full of apple orchards. In retrospect, it was silly of me to even think of calling them, but I got up my nerve and made one more attempt. I telephoned Franklyn Carlson, who, with his two brothers, owns the largest orchard in town. I drove by their farm almost daily on the way to take Ariel to her school bus. I felt shy about disturbing him, but I needed to talk to an apple expert. I needed to make this affirming first move.

Frank Carlson answered my call and told me to come by. I jumped in the car and drove straight over. Only when I started up the Carlson Orchard driveway, hearing the noise of the gravel grating under my car's tires, did my resolve begin to weaken. *Turn around. You're a pest. This is bad timing.* In fact, it was true. Towers of crates filled with freshly picked apples were visible in every direction. Frank was a mini-cyclone, answering his pager, cell phone, and loudspeaker calls. But he was kind, and he took time to chat with me in between answering questions coming at him from all sides. "Frank, where do I pull the tractor-trailer?"

"Frank, when does so-and-so pick up?" "How many bushels?" "What block are we picking first?"

It was Grand Central at rush hour.

I told him, "I purchased Art & Marie's Orchard on the other side of town. I'm thinking of bringing back the orchard and doing it organically."

Nodding, he replied. "I'm familiar with A & M Orchards. We don't grow any organic apples, but we press organic cider once a week with organic apples I have trucked in from Washington State. I have to pay as much for trucking as for the apples."

I nodded.

"A small organic operation might work," he continued.

"Would you buy some of our apples?" I asked.

"Hmm, I could do that."

I sensed in his response a sympathetic familiarity felt among anyone trying to grow apples in New England. Our humid climate makes it particularly difficult, unlike the dry air in Washington State, where apples are grown in a desert with little insect pressure. Though Frank and I didn't talk for long, I appreciated his encouragement.

I mentioned my plan to Ed, the neighbor who owns half the backhoe and whose house abuts the orchard. Ed is a retired executive, an avid outdoorsman, and a sailor. He had been pruning the trees closest to the edge of his property, even while the rest of the orchard declined.

Ed said, "The orchard was always a challenge for Art and Marie." And he too sounded that by now familiar warning. "It's really hard to grow apples."

Eager for a better sense of history, I asked him, "When did the Spauldings put in the orchard?"

"About twenty years ago. They cut down the forest, pulled out all the root systems, and graded the land. Carl did the bulldozing and clearing."

Carl Thompson, my neighbor on the other side of the pond, was a bit like Mike Mulligan and his steam shovel. He excavated every pond within twenty-five miles, created every golf course, and even built the local ski area, Nashoba Valley. He was a dowser, too, and people paid him to use his divining sticks to locate where to dig for water. By the time I met Carl he was in his eighties and cancer was ravaging one of his eyes. He refused treatment and kept to himself. I saw him outdoors every day sweeping the driveway and doing chores. I brought him raspberries and offered him eggs. He accepted the raspberries.

"I'll put them on my cereal."

"Don't you want any eggs?"

"No, I never cook. I eat my cereal in a bowl, and wipe it and the spoon clean with a paper towel."

A minimalist, I thought. *No cooking, no dirty dishes.*

"What do you eat for lunch?"

"My daughter brings me a sandwich every day. I eat a half for lunch and save the other half for dinner."

I continued to stop by and chat with Carl every week or so. He told me he mowed the field belonging to the Delaney Conservation Area alongside his property so the deer would have a field for grazing. He liked to watch them. Carl didn't seem to care if I was going to bring back the orchard. Carl was lonely and loved to chat. I urged him to stop by my shop sometime. I knew he did, because one day I found an oily wooden box outside the studio door filled with old bolts, heavy nuts, and metal parts he must have saved from bulldozer repairs. I figured he wanted to see for himself what I was up to. He always said to me, "You're the busiest person I know."

I did feel busy. I had my trio—my children, the farm, and the studio. I was dashing here and there, making up for the fact that all of my old identities had been taken away. I was no longer married and no longer a contributing member of a community that I cared about and who cared about me. Almost all of our mutual friends continued to support my former husband, Paul, which translated as not speaking to me. I missed the encouragement and support of my past familiar life. Paul would always happily machine parts for me or help with the engineering design for a sculpture. Now I had to do everything alone. In the studio I pushed myself to just do something, anything. The words *Beyond the Unknown* came to me. I trusted words.

For this new sculpture, I made a cloth-covered wall panel. I grabbed an interesting chunk of wood from the wood pile. It was a branch collar. A tree forms a branch collar when a branch is sawed off and the tree grows a raised callus of wood around the cut. Over time, the ring grows to cover the fresh wound. This large branch collar looked like a great "eye." The callus ring hadn't covered the large saw cut completely as it would on a smaller cut, and here I placed a gold-leafed seahorse as the iris for the "eye." Seahorses appealed to me not only for their resiliency (they move with ease while being knocked about by strong currents) but because Etienne Decroux, the father of French mime, and teacher of Marcel Marceau, is quoted as saying, "The more one looks at the seahorse, the more one is enthralled." I had spent two years studying mime in Paris in my early twenties. I had learned that Decroux believed mimes needed to move their spines with the articulation of a seahorse in order to portray a diversity of ages and characters. Like Decroux, I also thought seahorses were elegant and mysterious. To complete the piece, I used wire to attach hand-forged nails and write the words *Beyond the Unknown* on the cloth panel.

Beyond the Unknown spoke to me about finding a fulfilling life that I couldn't yet imagine. In placing the gold seahorse directly on the tree's wound, I was somehow healing it with seahorse magic. While I had no magic formula to bring the orchard back to life, my visit and conversation with Frank Carlson had given me hope. Growing apples became my new compass point. ❦

Row 4: Pruning for Light

Out of the blue, Marie Spaulding called.

"How are you doing with the orchard?" she asked.

"I've mowed and taken out the dead trees, pruned last winter, but again no crop. I don't know what else to do."

"I have a name of someone who might help. Denis Wagner. He used to manage the orchard at Nashoba Winery in Bolton."

"Great! Thank you. I'll call him."

On a November afternoon, Denis stopped by to talk. Though it was very cold, he was dressed in blue jeans, a sweatshirt, and green flannel vest. He had a ready smile—someone people are quickly drawn to.

"Do you want to see the orchard?"

We walked across the road and stopped in the middle of the first row of trees. I mentioned the varieties we had, remembering their names from the now disappeared map.

"See the smooth gray bark on that tree, Linda. It's a Cortland. You can also tell from the way it grows. Cortlands are tip bearers and their branches tend to hang down. When you prune them you have to make

Pruning in the orchard

cuts to lift the branches upwards. The weight of the apples will bring the limbs back down."

"The Macs fruit all along their branches," he said, grabbing a small one and pointing out the fruit buds spiraling along it.

"Like these?" I asked, pointing to a tight bud.

"No, those are leaf buds. The fruit buds are these larger ones. Sometimes it's hard to tell them apart." Peering around further he summed up, "Every fifth tree in this row is a Cortland. The rest are McIntosh."

"Denis," I said, unable to contain myself any longer. "I want to bring this orchard back to health and do it organically."

I saw a faint wrinkling around his eyes. Denis knew about the apple pests and diseases that plague the New England grower. He did not respond, "Oh, that's really hard."

He said, "Well, you can try."

We rambled through more rows, not saying much. The trees were still scraggly with lots of old wood. They spoke to Denis in a language I couldn't understand.

"What do you think?" I finally asked.

"We'll have to prune these trees heavily. Give me a call after the holidays, and we'll set a date to begin. I'll do some research on organic materials."

On a cold, sunny February afternoon, we began pruning together. Denis handed me one of the two leather scabbards with pruning saws he had brought with him. I clipped it to my belt. We each had our own hand clippers and long-handled loppers. Breaking through the crusty ice, our boots sank into the powdery snow underneath. We faced the first tree. My eyes followed along as Denis assessed the twists and turns, the weight and balance of old and new wood.

"Look for the leader," Denis instructed, "the main upward branch. Look for three tiers. You want to open the tree and make sure all branches receive light. If you don't prune correctly, the lower limbs will die back, and the tree will become umbrella-shaped, with no lower branches and very little fruiting wood."

I was trying to take this all in, while stamping my feet to keep warm. Denis was oblivious to the cold.

"Think of a Christmas tree shape with the top branches shorter, and the lower ones extending out further to receive light."

I tentatively lopped branches, one for every ten of Denis's cuts.

"This one?" I asked. Sometimes the response was yes. Other times he said, "No, take it back farther," pointing with his loppers. "There, where the branch splits. You don't want to leave a short spur sticking out." I did more looking than cutting.

Many of the trees were leaning far in one direction or were top-heavy. I saw a short, poorly developed branch sticking out from the center of a tree with a large limb directly above it.

Denis nodded as I took the saw from its leather sheath, anticipating my first large cut. The branch was almost four inches in diameter—an old elephant's trunk, with its downward curve and callused skin. It was in the top third of the tree, and Denis had explained that we remove wood here to rejuvenate the tree. I saw how difficult it was for the lower branch to grow shaded by the strong one above it.

Denis cautioned me, "Not too close to the tree or out so far out that you leave a stub."

I felt awkward. I didn't want the saw to slide out and scar the tree. But the pull of the stroke did the cutting and I adjusted to its rhythm. There is a breath to sawing, an ease as one lets the saw do the work. I was enjoying the graceful downward angle, but then the branch fell to the ground before I'd cut it off completely. The trunk frayed. Denis showed me how to prevent this by making a saw cut on the underside of the branch before beginning the next one. Lost in the strenuous work of sawing, I didn't think about how I had often sought out the shade of a strong branch. Embedded in my upbringing was a belief that others, and especially men, held the knowledge that I lacked. I didn't have confidence in myself. I would always, inevitably, doubt my own ability.

The strenuous sawing warmed my body, and I pulled off a layer and my wool hat.

Denis said. "A few large cuts are better than many small ones."

He was a natural among the trees. Trained as a ballet dancer, he now used his loppers to make staccato cuts—snip, snap, snip—in an almost musical, rhythmic way, then pulling out his saw, he would effortlessly slice through a large branch. I would drag the mass of woody stems from the center of the tree into the aisles, their raspy brittleness belying the dormant life inside.

Denis said cuts made to shorten a branch only invigorate growth. In response to snipping off the tip of a branch, a broom of new ones grows. So much to remember. I hesitated before making each cut, while Denis pruned with confidence from years of experience. As a sculptor I knew quite well when you remove wood you can't put it back. Pruning felt a lot like sculpting. There were these lovely moments after making a large cut and pulling the branches out from the tree when we would both smile. I couldn't explain it, but the tree looked better. More light, more air, happier, as if a great weight had been removed.

Once Denis surprised me, "Wait, don't remove all those suckers!" He was referring to the shoots growing thirty inches in one season, straight up from a branch. I was preparing to remove them all but he said, "We need to keep some of them. Those shoots will bear fruit in a couple of years." He grabbed a pliable tall stem, bent it down, and tucked it under another branch to keep it in place. On one tree I wanted to leave a branch growing in the wrong direction. It wasn't shading the lower story, and its fruit buds looked healthy. Denis agreed it was fine.

On the ground branches of all shapes and sizes lay discarded, half-buried in the snow. Death sentence and execution—flower buds along these branches would never become fruit. Denis would leave these massive tangles of branches for me to gather and burn once the pruning was over. It was an amazing amount of wood we removed. When I looked at the trees I felt like we had taken out too much. But Denis was the expert and I trusted him. Pruning to encourage each tree to reach its fullest potential meant removing a lot of unnecessary wood.

This metaphor wasn't lost on me. I had given up a lot to change my life. I asked him, "What happens if we don't prune?"

"You get a crop the first year and even for a few successive years. But when the trees are left over many years—which is your situation—there's a lot of wood to remove.

"They have been fighting to survive," I surmised.

Denis nodded. "You're bringing the trees back to a balance between fruitful and vegetative growth."

After our first week of pruning Denis suggested a morning drive to view other orchards. I climbed into his gray pickup truck.

"Look at those trees," he said, pointing.

"I'm not sure what I'm looking at," I replied leaning out of the passenger window.

"Those are dwarf apple trees supported by a trellis of wires."

"Why the wires?"

"Dwarf trees are weakly rooted and need the support."

"How many trees are there? How much fruit can you get off those little trees?"

"One thousand dwarf trees to an acre. More fruit than an acre of standard size trees."

"These apples look like rows of grapes," I said.

I knew grapes climb up trees and branches, and range over stone walls, covering vast areas. It's only in commercial production grapes are grown on wires in neat rows, pruned to just a few new shoots each year.

Seeing the apples so civilized, I realized the next generation might not know apples once grew on trees.

Denis drove us back to the farm and we resumed pruning. I climbed to the top of a tree to cut back the central leader. From sixteen feet high, I had a bird's-eye view over the rows of trees sloping towards the wetlands. I saw them like calligraphy flowing down a page, a poem written in the landscape. Looking straight down into the tree, the branches radiated outwards like the spokes of a wheel. I felt a strange peacefulness sitting so high—positioned as if in the center of creation.

When I climbed down, Denis asked, "Do you like it up there?"

"Yes, it's beautiful."

We listened together to the bluebirds chattering in the bright, wintry light. I hadn't realized they stayed up north all winter. From the other side of the road, a raucous medley of geese honks and chicken squawks told us there must be an intruder. Maybe a hawk or some other raptor? Then, just as quickly, the clamor hushed.

Our pruning in the orchard took two weeks. I was a little sad when it was over. I enjoyed the companionable work. I was learning that pruning is not only about structure and form, but meeting each tree's particular strength and weakness. Some tend to be upright, others produce droopy branches. Some are wildly enthusiastic growers, while others develop slowly. As we walked along the pruned trees, I felt a longing to nurture them. Denis said, "Like your children," as if he knew what I was thinking.

After our pruning the orchard looked skeletal. I was in awe that these spindly branches might someday hold fruit. The transformation seemed improbable, but Denis didn't doubt we would have apples. ❦

Row 5: Kyoto, Japan

The farm needed a new name. I didn't want to use A & M Orchards. Art had explained to me he'd gone to the Town Hall to register the farm as a business and the Town Clerk had asked for the farm's name. Off the cuff, he had replied, A & M Orchards, for Art and Marie. I decided to change its name to **Old Frog Pond Farm** after the haiku by the seventeenth-century Japanese Zen poet Bashō. This name connected me back to the haiku poets I had been introduced to in Kyoto, Japan.

> old pond
>
> frog jumps
>
> splash of water
>
> —Matsuo Bashō

At Bryn Mawr College near Philadelphia, where I studied fine arts and poetry, I also performed as one member of the duet the **Mudhead Mimes**, named after the Mudheads, Pueblo Indian clowns. The Pueblo Indian clowns took clowning seriously. They had a role to play in the

With Noh Sensei, Kyoto, Japan

society by poking fun at wrongdoers and showing the importance of moral values to ensure the flourishing of the community. Their name, **Mudhead**, came from the colorful earthen clay they used to paint their faces.

My Mudhead Mimes performing career was outside the college curriculum, and before graduation I applied for a Thomas J. Watson Fellowship to continue this exploration of mime and theater in Japan with a Noh Theater actor.

Noh is a thirteenth-century Zen art that combines poetry, dance, music, and mime. Noh actors wear stylized wooden masks, carved and painted to express different emotional states. I hoped training in the Noh Theater would teach me to express deeper emotions I longed to share in performance. I was awarded the fellowship and after graduation left for Kyoto. It was there that I was introduced to Bashō's poetry.

I arrived alone in Kyoto in September 1979 without knowing any Japanese. How do I get anywhere? Where do I eat? How do I use the public baths? One sympathetic contact I met through a mutual friend in the States made this foreign life possible. Judith, a professor and student of the Noh Theater, had lived in Kyoto for ten years. She found me a place to live in Chion-In, a temple near Kyoto University. Traditional Japanese rooms are measured in tatami mat sizes: a typical room might be six mats, a tea room is usually four mats with an additional half-mat opening in the center for the brazier. My one-mat room, the smallest possible, and the only one available, meant I rolled out my sleeping bag for sleeping and rolled it back up in the morning to sit and eat breakfast. It was cheap and would make my fellowship funds last.

The walls were thin and I didn't feel any separation from the outdoors. Mosquitos buzzed around my head and dogs barked outside the window. Every day, before dawn and in the early evening, I heard mysterious chanting coming from the largest temple building. The monks were reciting the liturgy for morning and evening services. These ancient guttural sounds reverberated inside my body.

An old maple tree outside my room had a hollow half-shell for its trunk with only a single branch still alive. An intricate scaffolding of bamboo and rope supported the branch. This maple tree made me think about nature in a new way. Not only did I marvel at the meticulous care provided by the gardener, but the tree's tenacity to survive expressed a depth of beauty I recognized as a fundamental truth. As I visited more of the famous sites and gardens in Kyoto, the traditional Zen poets, like Bashō, became my companions. Their poetry taught me a new way of appreciating the natural world. A black crow landing on a branch shook down a shiver of snow. A camelia flower didn't age and release its faded blossom petals one by one, but fell off the twig, whole and complete.

Judith arranged an introduction with a Noh teacher she thought might be willing to teach me. On the day of our meeting with Takabayshi Sensei, we walked down a narrow path, entering the rear of his house through a small sliding door. We sat in a small tatami mat room to wait for him, kneeling in *seiza* position, with our legs tucked underneath us. A highly polished wood stage was in front of us, and the walls and ceiling were also dark with smooth wood. Takabayshi Sensei came in and knelt down, his silk kimono and *hakama*, oversized pants worn over a kimono, rustling. We bowed to him and he bowed. I was overwhelmed by the quiet of this first meeting, the intimacy of being somewhere so different, so private. Judith and Sensei chatted in Japanese while I sat and smiled. She explained my background in theater and mime, and Takabayashi told her he would teach me. He beamed when he spoke and I was captivated. I would have my lessons at seven o'clock in the morning. Judith lent me an old blue bicycle to ride the five miles from my room in eastern Kyoto west to Toji-in. The bike was stuck in third gear, but I didn't care.

On my first lesson day, I slipped into the side door, put on my new bright white *tabi* (fitted white toe socks) and knelt to wait. Sensei came in and sat in front of me. We bowed. He gave me a practice fan with blue clouds, the fan of the Kita School, the Noh Theater school he belonged to. I followed him onto the stage, where we both knelt side by side. He said something in Japanese I didn't understand.

With closed fan in my right hand, out of the corner of my eye I watched his movements and followed along. We slowly stood, then slid left foot, then right, then left, then the right foot even further forward while pointing ahead with the right arm holding the closed fan. Then left foot back, right foot back, and left arm meeting right arm and both opening widely. We closed our arms and knelt down. That was my first lesson, pointing, opening, and closing—the beginning of the dance in the Noh play *Yuya*. The play is about a young woman who longs to return to her home where her mother is ill. The powerful man she serves, Lord Munemori, wants to enjoy cherry blossom viewing with her and denies her request. She reluctantly dances at the cherry blossom party, and when some blossoms fall, she is so moved she takes a strip of paper from the sleeve of her kimono, writes and then recites a poem about a falling blossom, in reality a poem about her dying mother. Moved by the love she expresses for her mother, the lord relents and allows his mistress to return home. The patterns were simple enough, but the plight of this young woman moved my heart. I felt her struggle. I identified with her powerlessness.

Takabayashi knew it would soon be cold. Kyoto is known for both its humid heat in summer and wet, stinging cold in winter. Traditional houses have little heat and no insulation. He had his daughter sew me a warm wool kimono, and I bought a pair of *hakama* pants to wear for each lesson. For several weeks Sensei had to tie the complex of knots for my hakama pants, around, over and under, helping me as if I was his daughter. After our lesson, I folded my kimono and hakama along the exact same fold lines and enclosed it in a scarf leaving it in a low cabinet near the stage.

After several months of lessons, I performed this dance at an informal recital with a few of Takabayashi Sensei's other students. For the performance, he put a screen in the back of the stage with an ink painting of a pine tree. An old gnarly pine is painted on the wall behind every Noh stage and is said to be the eternal backdrop of Noh. It serves as a reminder that the Noh was originally performed outdoors, for the gods. A pine tree from the Kasuga Shrine in Nara is said to be the inspiration for it.

After this performance I wrote in my journal, "Perhaps Noh is not acting." I always wanted to know the words I was dancing, the story line of the play, but it was becoming clear the only thing Takabayashi wanted me to do was execute the exact patterns he was teaching. I was to do them in the clearest and most straightforward way I could. I wasn't to think about the words of the play, or that I was acting the part of *Yuya*. Takabayashi was only interested in the movements and the rhythm. I had entered a training where I was being taught not to express my own self-expression. Ironically, I had wanted to study Noh Theatre to find tools to share more deeply my longings and suffering, but I was being taught to do the opposite.

A year and a half into my training, Judith told me about a visitor she was expecting, Paul Matisse, a friend of hers from Cambridge, Massachusetts, an inventor and the grandson of the French artist Henri Matisse. On a Sunday afternoon I came by Judith's place after seeing a Noh performance, rang the bell and entered. I saw Judith's friend sitting at a low table near the shoji screens in front of the garden. My first impression was his seriousness: he was bent over his book and didn't look up. In the kitchen, Judith was chopping vegetables and she handed me greens to wash. Only when the three of us sat down to eat at the low table was I introduced. I smiled, Paul smiled, and Judith asked about the Noh performance I had been to that afternoon. Just as we were about to begin our meal, her phone rang and she got up to answer. The phone conversation in Japanese went on and on. I wondered why she didn't hang up as Paul and I sat awkwardly waiting for her return. He began to eat, and to be polite, I followed his lead.

When Judith finally returned, she was pleased we had started to eat without her. The meal ended shortly afterwards with Paul going back to his book. I followed Judith to the kitchen to help wash dishes.

"Would you take Paul on a few sightseeing trips?"

He was supposed to have come a month earlier, but delays in a sculpture project, *The Musical Fence*, had forced him to postpone his trip. Judith's school was back in session, and she had classes to prepare and teach.

"I'd be happy to take him to a few places. I'll think of something."

After more talk about the Noh performance, I went home.

Two days later I telephoned Judith's house at nine in the morning. I had never visited the small temple Jakko-in north of Kyoto, and was reading a Noh play that took place there. I thought it would make an interesting day trip for her houseguest.

Paul answered the phone.

"Hello. It's Linda. Would you like to go with me to Ohara?"

"I have no plans for the day."

"Then meet me at Demachi Yanagi Station on Imadegawa Street." I knew it would be easy for him to find on a map.

Paul was in his mid-forties, tall with hazel eyes and thinning reddish hair. As we rode the train together, he asked about the Noh theater and I shared my love for this practice.

"I'll never become a professional Noh performer," I said. "That requires either decades of study or being born into a Noh family. But I love the intense beauty of the plays, the dance, and the poetry. I'm really drawn to the single-minded effort and discipline Noh training requires." What I didn't share was how easy I found it to follow my teacher's instructions. While in my little tatami mat room, I created mime sketches and wrote stories. These were self-referential, and I struggled with them. It was easier to be part of a tradition than create my own artistic language.

Forty minutes later, Paul and I left the train and walked up the road, stopping to watch the women harvesting and tying bundles of rice. They wore traditional farmer's cotton ikat clothing, loose pants and a matching short kimono-like work jacket tied with a sash. Their hair was tied up in printed kerchiefs. I tried to memorize the patterns of their movements—cutting the canes, wrapping bunches together, and making neat piles.

Heading uphill on a narrow road Paul and I came to the small temple, the Jakko-in. Here the widowed Empress Kenreimon-in lived out her days praying for her deceased family after its defeat in the famous naval battle of 1185 described in the classic epic *The Tale of Genji*. Samurais as well as the ruling family tried to drown themselves rather than be taken prisoner. Kenreimon-in was dragged out of the waves by her long hair. Later she shaved her head and became a nun. I easily imagined her sitting under the cherry trees contemplating the impermanence of life. Later I sent Paul this poem about our visit.

Ohara Visit

Two strangers on a pilgrimage to the Jakko-in
(The temple of the Empress Kenreimon-in
who retreated from life after the Gempei War)

Climbed the stone steps from the valley up the hill
Through the shadows and cypress roots

Stopped in front of a cherry tree trunk
Half-buried beneath the unswept moss

Stood outside of the wooden shrine
Where Kenreimon-in prayed for her defeated clan

Remained inside the memory of the day
Until they bowed and broke the silence.

Paul told me on our return from Ohara that he would like to go to Ise, Japan's most treasured Shinto shrine. We made a plan to travel through the Wakayama prefecture, an area known for its hot springs, and then visit Ise. A few days later we boarded a bus from Kyoto Station. I had packed two apples and offered him one. With his ebony handled pocketknife, Paul cut one of the apples in two. But not crosswise or lengthwise—he formed a complex interlocking shape, and held out both parts for me to choose one. I picked the one with the stem.

I ate mine, and Paul said, "You ate the core."

"Yes," I replied. I didn't want to tarnish the moment by holding an apple core that would only turn brown. Paul's expression of marvel wasn't lost on me. Then he reached over and took the stem from my hand.

We got off the bus on the bridge at Unamine Hot Springs. Stone steps led down to a platform with two large basins built into the river. These pools were filled directly from the spring and the temperature was near boiling. Here the village women left bags of eggs and carrots to cook while they washed themselves in the nearby public baths.

We watched people dressed in blue and white kimonos and *geta* (wooden shoes) shuffle up and down the street. They seemed to be coming from the Azumaya Hotel. We walked up to the inn, asked to stay overnight, and were led into a second-floor room. The young Japanese woman opened the *shoji*, the sliding panel to the outdoors, and the room filled with the gushing sound of water. She pointed to two low chairs on the window terrace, left us, and quickly returned with tea. Another whooshing sound. She had opened wide the bath faucets and was filling the tub. We didn't know who would take the first bath, she didn't know we were strangers.

I came out of the bath in my cotton kimono with my braid untied, long brown hair down to my waist. Paul looked astonished since he had only seen it tied up in a braided bun. After his bath we paraded around town like the other visitors in our kimonos, walking across the river, and following a stream. As we climbed up the trail, we passed one waterfall after another and stopped at a mountain pool.

"I have to go in," Paul said, as he took off his kimono. I followed him into the freezing water. Then we sat on a large flat rock and felt the warmth of the stone and warmer water gently flowing over it. We stood to leave and Paul leaned over, lifting me off the ground in an embrace.

Back at the inn the maid brought our dinner, covering the table with myriad small dishes of vegetables, fish, and rice. We sat in our kimonos, sipping sake, and listening to the sound of falling water. It was too early to go to bed. Paul opened the faucets to fill our tub. The great rushing water resounded again through the room. When the tub was full he invited me to share his bath.

The next day we traveled to Nachi Falls, for centuries a destination for seekers and pilgrims. The white threads of water fell more than four hundred feet out of a primeval forest. After Nachi we took the train to Ise, the birthplace of the gods. We walked through the sites of the twin shrines, learning how the Japanese builders completely rebuild the temple on an alternate site every twenty years, a tradition that goes back to the seventh century. In this way, each generation learns the ancient construction skills necessary to rebuild.

At the entrance to the shrine, Paul clapped loudly to get the attention of the gods. Then he pulled the heavy jute rope, ringing a bell, and tossed a few coins into a wood-slatted box. Paul had been to Japan a number of years earlier so he knew what to do. The new shrine buildings lacked the patina of age, but the surrounding forest of Cryptomeria trees more than made up for it. Straight and tall, their presence conveyed solemnity. The Japanese consider these hundred-year-old trees to be the true home of the Gods. Thick red ropes around their trunks mark them as sacred.

Our trip ended at the train station in Kyoto. I had an English lesson to teach that evening and a Noh dance to practice for a recital in Tokyo the following weekend. We had shared the mysterious Japanese world of beauty and power, myth and legend. After Paul's two-week Kyoto visit, he returned to Cambridge. Before the next week had ended, I received four letters and had written three. A courtship of daily letters, drawings, and poems across the Pacific followed. Paul was excited to hear more about my training. He loved reading my ideas and descriptions of dances and gardens. We wrote letters to each other every day and our relationship deepened over the next four months.

Then Paul suggested we meet halfway and spend ten days together in Hawai'i. It was a time of blue water, sun, and sand, lovemaking, generous food and wine. Two days before our vacation ended, Paul asked, "Will you come live with me in my loft in Cambridge?"

I was twenty-four. Paul was forty-seven, with four children. His oldest was twenty and the youngest fourteen. I didn't think about our age difference or about getting along with his kids. I didn't think about leaving the independent life I had created. I said *yes* without hesitation. I didn't know what life with Paul would be like, but I couldn't imagine life without him. I was in love with this creative and sensitive man. I believed that with Paul my life would expand in ways I couldn't yet imagine.

Noh theater is a lifelong commitment, an artistic and spiritual path that offers much in return for constancy and dedication. I hadn't planned to train for the rest of my life, though without meeting Paul, I don't know what would have tempted me to leave. I flew back from Hawai'i to Kyoto excited about our future together, but also concerned about what to tell my Noh teacher.

At my next lesson with Takabayashi I told him I had fallen in love. I was going to leave Japan. He had been a devoted teacher and I had been a devoted student, but I had been blindsided by this fledgling love.

"When will you go?" he asked, his eyes wide with surprise.

"Soon," I stammered. It was late December.

Without much hesitation he said, "How about May? I will teach you the *maibayashi* Noh dance for *Hagoromo*. You can perform it in Osaka before you leave."

I didn't follow my desire to return to the States right away. I stayed to do what my teacher asked. We would formally mark the completion of our training together. I worked hard memorizing the dance and the music, as it would be my most challenging performance. I had never danced with hired musicians, only with Takabayashi chanting while keeping the beat with his closed fan. Not many foreigners perform *maibayashi*. I only remember the ending of my performance—I finished a few seconds early and stood still, stricken with a self-conscious unease while the drums continued.

"What happened?" Takabayashi asked me after the drummers had packed up and left.

"I don't know," I said.

"You forgot the last twirl, the rising up to heaven."

I had already been lifted into a different life.

I was going to live with Paul. ❦

Row 6: What's in a Name?

When I flew back from Japan to move in with Paul, I carried a suitcase of clothes, my Noh kimono, fans, books, notebooks—everything I owned. In Japan I'd taught mime and English, but I didn't know what I would do back in America or how I would use my Noh training in my new life. I'd spent two years immersed in the world of Noh Theater and traditional Japan. How would it manifest? I didn't know but I was eager to plunge ahead.

In New York City I stayed overnight with my mother. Paul would meet us in the morning. Over breakfast, before he arrived, she asked, "Will you come down to New York?" I looked at her questioningly. "Maybe take a class?" she prompted.

My mother was worried about what I was going to do in Cambridge with Paul. My unconventional mother who was never waiting on the front step when I came home from school or attended a school play, visited me in Kyoto a month after Paul's visit. As luck would have it, she had been presenting a paper at an anthropology conference in Vladivostok, in the Soviet Union, and stopped in Japan before returning home.

Two Herons, watercolor, 2019

She had seen Paul's thick airmail envelopes arrive sometimes two in the same day. She felt my excitement and didn't hide her own. Paul was clearly enchanted with me, and I was growing increasingly attached to this relationship through our letters. But she had also questioned our age difference, and asked what I would do if I returned to the States to live with him.

Now, in her New York City apartment, I knew she was asking if I would continue to live independently, to follow the arc of my own life. Shy and sensitive, I was only beginning to find my own voice. She was worried I wouldn't be able to establish my own identity in a relationship with a brilliant man twenty-three years my senior, with four children and a legacy of modern art.

My mother, Annette Weiner, was then Chair of the Anthropology Department at New York University. She considered it important for women to have their own income and create their own paths. She had been raised in West Philadelphia, an older sister to three younger brothers. She went to Girls High School, the best public school in the city, and graduated with honors. Teachers urged her to consider college, but her parents said no; she should find a suitable vocation, marry, settle down, and have children. She became an X-ray technician, married my father, a pharmacist, had two children, and worked in his drugstore.

Her parents had thwarted her effort to go to college and, in her words, become somebody. Unhappy in her life, and with the encouragement of a therapist, she enrolled as an undergraduate at the University of Pennsylvania when I was nine and my brother was six. I remember bold abstract canvases—she was taking a painting class, and one of her art professors was teaching in the style of Hans Hoffmann. Then she discovered the book *Stranger and Friend: The Way of the Anthropologist* by Hortense Powdermaker.

In 1929, Powdermaker was the first female anthropologist to study a primitive culture in Melanesia, the area that includes Papua New Guinea and many small island chains. Powdermaker's book includes personal experiences of what it was like to do fieldwork. I still have my mother's hardback copy with a slightly torn paper dust jacket and her pen markings.

Anthropology was a bold frontier, especially for women. The idea of traveling to a remote place must have appealed to her. My mother changed her major from fine arts and received her B.A. in cultural anthropology. She wanted to continue studying at Penn, but the department deemed her an "older" woman with no real academic future. Fortunate to find a different attitude at Bryn Mawr College, she received her Ph.D. in 1974, the year I graduated from high school. I knew she was worried about my moving in with Paul, but that morning in her apartment we didn't talk about it.

Paul had driven into the city the night before and stayed with his father uptown. He would be meeting us shortly. When he arrived at the apartment, the three of us had a quick cup of coffee. He was eager to get on the road, so I gathered my belongings and we took the elevator down to the street level. I remember watching the floors go by, standing between my mother and my lover. My last New York moment was the sound of her high-heel shoes clicking along the north side of Washington Square as she headed towards her office, the entry marked by two stone lions. Even today, when I am in the square, I hear her heels, her confidence. She had style and personal power. With great perseverance she had created a life for herself that was deeply satisfying.

I moved into Paul's loft in Kendall Square in Cambridge, not knowing anyone in the city. We weren't supposed to be living there—the place had been the manufacturing space for an invention of Paul's, small objects known as *Kalliroscope* viewers. These rectangular devices, filled with liquid, exhibited beautiful patterns and demonstrated the physics of fluid flow. Even though he was no longer making *Kalliroscope* viewers, he used the shop to work on other inventions and had made a home for himself there after his first marriage ended.

We had a small kitchen, a living area, and four infrared heat lamps in the bedroom over the bed. Our shower was in one side of a double stainless steel mop sink. At 4 p.m. on Fridays the heat would go off, and it wouldn't come back on until Mondays at 5 a.m.

One evening I told Paul I didn't particularly like my last name, Weiner. Too many memories of childhood teasing—*Oscar Meyer Weiner* hotdogs and worse. And how could I like Weiner when I was with a Matisse?

Paul said, "Why not change it?"

I immediately thought of the traditional Japanese poets who took pen names. Bashō, the haiku poet, published poetry using three different names. His birth name, Sobo, he used while he was a young page in the service of a samurai lord. Then, after Bashō's youthful master died, he left the samurai world, and wandered to different cities, studying and writing verse. With the publication of several poems and some acceptance by the literary world, he gave himself a new name, Tosei. Later, his students built their teacher a small rustic hut and one of them planted a banana tree by it. The residence became known as Bashō (banana plant) Hut, and eventually his name came to be Bashō.

The idea of taking a new name as I was beginning a new life appealed to me. I thought of a poetic last name like "River," but Paul was quick to say, "No. That sounds like a Hollywood name. It should be a normal name." He pulled out the Manhattan phone book, opened it at random to the H's, and found Hoffman.

I knew my mother would accept the name change. It wouldn't matter to her. She had already been through one name change with me. I was born Linda Bess Weiner. When I was a child I disliked my middle name; it seemed so old-fashioned. I got the sense my mother didn't really like it either. The name came from my father's mother, an overbearing woman. I imagine my mother must have felt pressured to do what her mother-in-law wanted. When I was about ten, my mother said, "If you don't like your middle name, give yourself a new one." We decided to change it to Elizabeth. The initials, LEW, had a nice ring to them, and she gave me a necklace with those letters. We didn't say anything to my grandmother. A few years later, it all seemed false, so I simply dropped having a middle name.

However, I felt uncomfortable about how my father might feel. He was living in Philadelphia with his new wife. He wouldn't have any idea why I would even think of a name change.

I felt awkward about all of this, and didn't particularly like Hoffman, but Paul assured me, that was then and this was now, and it didn't matter. I didn't know how to verbalize my discomfort, or speak up for myself, so I took up Hoffman, going with him to the Cambridge courthouse, and changed my name officially, a declaration I no longer belonged to my family of origin. I was a new person without a family history.

When I suggested I find a part-time job, Paul said, "That's not necessary." He wanted to support me in finding a new path for my art. Bursting with enthusiasm for the Noh theater, I wanted to share its beauty and poetry. But Noh theater cannot be performed alone, and I had only studied for two years. I thought I might try to meet some modern dancers and possibly work with them. Together Paul and I cleared a back room in the loft and put down vinyl squares for flooring so I would have a practice room. He even made me a large mirror using heat-shrinkable mylar stretched over wood frames. He was generous and loving in his support of me and I was grateful.

With Christmas approaching, and without money to buy Paul a gift, I decided to make him one. I used some white homespun cloth I found in the loft. I covered a wood panel with the cloth and wrote the words *The Line Never Ceases to Meet* with cloth-covered copper wire, giving a tactile expression to the haiku-like poem I had written. I loved seeing the words in cloth and made a second poem using the same white cloth: *The Moon Reflects Over and Over on Snow.*

Then I decided to find more cloth and add color and texture. I took over the dance room Paul had given me for movement and worked every day on new poems in cloth. Being creative grounded me, and Paul loved that I was inspired by our happiness together. It was an artistically fertile time. I was being supported and had no family obligations. We lived simply in small rooms and I could work every day in the studio we had made together.

That summer we visited his mother, Teeny, in her farmhouse outside Paris. She always invited artists to her home for dinners and longer visits. When we were there, John Cage was a houseguest, and we played chess together on a set designed by Alexander Calder. Nicki de Saint Phalle stopped by for drinks, and artist friends Claude and Francois LaLanne lived in a neighboring town. Teeny had a treasured Brancusi sculpture in one corner, a Jasper Johns print on the wall, and a small Colima pottery dog on the coffee table. I didn't belong among these luminaries. I was an ordinary gal, born in a working-class town, with a pharmacist father. My mother had made a different life for herself, but I hadn't done that yet. Only the fact I was with Paul made my presence explainable. I hadn't earned my entrée.

We were invited to attend an opening at the Pompidou Center for the video artist Nam June Paik. I had nothing appropriate to wear, having brought only a few pairs of jeans and shirts.

Teeny said, "Come upstairs with me."

From one of her closets, she pulled a yellow Moroccan outfit with a long tunic and pants. "Here, try it on. I think it will fit you."

"Perfect," she said, as she went over to her bureau to get the silvery bell-shaped buttons to close the opening at the neck.

I looked in the mirror, and though I was grateful to have something to wear, I was a doll dressed up in a costume.

We drove to Paris later in the evening. At the museum people spoke excitedly with each other while I stood off to one side. I spoke casually with Nam June Paik. I was enjoying myself until he sweetly asked, "Is Paul your father?" I did look terribly young with my long dark braid. It was an innocent mistake, but his question made me feel inconsequential.

When we got back to Teeny's, I said to Paul, "Nam June asked if you were my father. I felt so uncomfortable."

"Don't worry," he said. "It's not important." And he put his arm around my shoulder to comfort me.

But it was important to me. Nam June's comment had touched the heart of my being. I was not comforted. No longer was I independent and autonomous. Clearly I had been seen as an appendage. Nam June Paik's question reinforced my sense of being an imposter. I felt naked to the core. A shy girl falls in love with a man much older, who happens to belong to a legacy of great artists. Nothing was inherently wrong with any of these conditions, or with Nam June's innocent question, yet I failed to anticipate their corrosive long-term effects.

The next day, I put the Moroccan outfit back on a hanger and gave it to Teeny. "Oh, no," she said. "You must take it with you. It no longer fits me."

Paul and I returned to Cambridge. I was still bothered by Nam June's question. I had given up my life in the Noh Theater and the expat world of Kyoto. I knew only those people Paul introduced me to in Cambridge. Most of them were older, his intimate community. I was an outsider, but since I was with Paul, they, of course, wanted to get to know me.

Forty years later, I have not given away the Moroccan outfit. It still hangs in an extra closet. I even have the small bell buttons. I don't know how to let it go. Not that I give it much thought. Years go by and I forget about it, but then I see it in that extra closet. I certainly will never pass it on to someone else saying it no longer fits. ✻

Row 7: The Church, Groton, Massachusetts

Paul wanted to look for a place to live outside the city, a barn where we could both have workshops and a small living space. We drove through central Massachusetts looking for barns for sale, but barns in New England are either rickety structures built to cover the hay, or they are beautiful, and come with attached farmhouses and land. We neither needed nor could afford one of those grand properties. Then on a discouraging return trip from southern New Hampshire we drove by a small *For Sale* sign outside a white clapboard church on Main Street in Groton, Massachusetts.

The Baptist parishioners had abandoned the building several years earlier to build a bigger church for their growing congregation. It was on the market for a song since it had no parking and was, for most people, a white albatross. Paul wanted to offer one dollar to take it off their hands. We eventually paid $40,000 for it. In January 1983, we celebrated our purchase of the church, Paul's fiftieth birthday, and our marriage. I changed my surname to Matisse. Paul thought given the difference in our ages it would be good for me to share his last name so

Pines and Sargasso Sea, poems in cloth, 1993

I would be recognized as his wife. I kept Hoffman as my artist name to identify my independence as an artist.

That winter the building proved cold and drafty, but we had a full-immersion baptismal font, a black Garland six-burner cook stove, and men's and women's bathrooms with enough toilets for a large congregation. We planned someday to transform this great ark into our home, with bedrooms, a living room, and a real kitchen.

Soon I was pregnant. Even though Paul already had four children, I never doubted we would have children together. I knew he loved his older children, he loved me, and I assumed he would want us to have children. Paul was amazed as he participated in each birth and we both fell in love with our babies—Alexander born in 1984, Nicholas in 1987, and Ariel in 1989.

I poured myself into our young children's lives. The Baptist Church sanctuary became the children's vast unheated playroom. Paul hung a swing from the twenty-foot ceiling. As the children grew, he added carabiners on the rope ends so they could exchange the swing for rings or a bar, and attempt all kinds of acrobatics. Ariel would put on rollerblades and pads, and skate around and around the big room in a black leotard and crash helmet. I planned and prepared for holidays, and we always had his four older children to share in the festivities. George was at the University of Massachusetts in Amherst. He loved old cars and drove a beat-up Chevy. We once borrowed it, and beforehand, he had to show Paul how you had to stop driving and do something underneath to put it in reverse. Michael, who lived in Cambridge, had an uncanny knack for impersonating everyone, and always kept us laughing. Robert, nicknamed Robin, a senior at the Cambridge Friends School, would be attending the University of Massachusetts in the fall. The youngest, Sophie, was a charming animal lover and already a gifted artist.

On Christmas Eve, Alex followed Paul up the steeple staircases and rickety ladders to the belfry, opened a louver for Santa Claus, and hung the stockings on the church bell. In the morning they repeated the climb to find the filled stockings. Paul's older children arrived after having had breakfast with their mother in Cambridge. The young children idolized the older ones, and the older ones were very sweet with their half brothers and sister. They accepted me readily into the family and I loved them—love them still.

My passion for making *Poems in Cloth* shifted to work in three dimensions. I started to use larger objects—a paint brush, old bottles, and tree branches. Paul worked long hours experimenting with aluminum kinetic sculptures with wildly waving arm weights and spinning disks. In the dark, tiny lights at the ends of the spinning arms revealed astonishing patterns, as the bright lights left trails on your retina.

Paul took pleasure in solving problems and designing solutions. From a young age he was always making things. After graduating from Harvard University, he attended the university's Graduate School of Design, studying to be an architect, but then changed his focus and took a job as a designer/inventor at Arthur D. Little, a Cambridge research and design firm. When I wanted to attach an oyster shell to one of my panels, he made a little aluminum piece to screw the delicate shell to the cloth covered board. From the front, the shell appeared to be floating. He then made fifty of these devices so I could make a *Poem in Cloth* using saved oyster shells from oysters we had eaten together.

He asked his daughter, Sophie, to draw a picture of two geese flying which he transferred to aluminum and had gold-leafed, a weather vane for the church steeple, a symbol of the two of us flying together.

For the next ten years the children, my art, and volunteer community work filled my life. In summer, we traveled with the younger children to France to visit Paul's mother. We spent a few long weekends in northern Vermont where my mother stayed over academic vacations with her new husband, William (Bill) Mitchell, also an anthropologist. In winter we sledded on the big hill behind Lawrence Academy, built snowmen and tree forts, and went on a few ski vacations with Paul's older children. We had had little money when I first met Paul, but in 1989, his father died, and Paul's inheritance made such luxuries possible.

In the fall I took our children apple picking at a nearby farm where we joined large crowds from Boston, their cars packed for a day in the country. An officer directed traffic at the street crossing as tractors pulled hay wagons filled with families to different blocks of the orchard. Long lines formed at the farmstand counters, and customers paid for peck and half-bushel bags before they headed down the rows for picking. We always climbed to the top of the hill to pick our apples and made applesauce when we got home. When the Rosenberger orchard closed a few years later, a melancholic blanket covered the hillside. I drove by often and felt the sad weight of the old trees as they stood one year, then two, then three without being pruned. No longer were there white clouds of flowers in spring, or red fruit pulling down the branches in the fall.

What was happening in Groton was no different than a trend seen all over the country. In 1950 there were 5.6 million farms and by 2008 the number was 2.2 million, a staggering tsunami of change. In 2008, the American Farmland Trust was created to protect farmland and help farmers keep their farms. In 2012, they issued a report, *Farms Under Threat: The State of America's Farmland*. It showed that ninety-one percent of places that grow fruits, tree nuts, and berries are "directly in the path of development."

Living in rural New England in the nineties I had a front-row seat to witness the disappearance of farmland from the landscape. The vanishing happened as quickly as a magician's trick. An apple orchard became *Orchard Lane* with twenty-five new houses. A dairy farm became *Easy Acres*, a subdivision with forty duplexes.

When something disturbs me, it settles into my unconscious and before long I find it appearing in my art. I decided to make a sculpture using old agricultural tools. I put an ad in our local newspaper: *Artist looking for old agricultural tools for an artwork about the disappearance of farmland.* From one small notice in the Groton Herald the phone started to ring. People responded with warmth and generosity. Usually it was a single tool, a saw that had belonged to a grandfather, a scythe, or a treasured rake. One man offered me rough-sawn boards with sinuous edges.

In little time, I had a collection of tools that evoked human effort, the sweat and muscle of hand labor. The first tool I worked with was a heavy pitchfork. With the muted colors of Shaker tape, the remnant material I had been gifted from the Shaker Workshop Factory, I wove cloth bands through the tines of the fork. I wrote a poem to accompany the sculpture.

> the weaving
> of fields
>
> ancestry
> creation
>
> autumn grasses
>
> scatterfallen
> seeds

I was a "tree hugger." I hated to see trees taken down along town roads. I bemoaned electric wires cutting through the butchered tree canopies. One great tree on the common near the Nashua River had a large painted orange 'X' on it. The next day, I went with a friend and we spray-painted the 'X' brown to match the bark. The state highway men drove right by it.

For the next sculpture, *Marked Trees*, I used a five-foot saw blade with a mosaic of sharp teeth, a gift from a veterinarian. I added bands of green cloth and long slivers of sawn wood to the panel.

> green woods
> old pasture
> buried rust
>
> the saw sharp
> silence
> of marked trees

I wanted to save more trees, farmland, and open space. Saving a woodlot is relatively easy. You can cut a few trails and let the trees grow naturally. Saving a farm is not as simple. Someone has to live on or near the land and work it. The farms and farmers were disappearing.

From the outside I had a picture-book marriage, a beautiful life, and help with the children. Paul and I had back-to-back studios on the ground floor. The architecture of our home determined that Paul and I physically shared almost every free moment. We lived and worked in the same place. We ate three meals a day together. Our shower was built with two showerheads, one on each side, his higher, and mine lower. The Japanese soaking tub Paul designed fit the two of us perfectly. Paul loved to do everything beautifully and meticulously, and he was ready to do anything and everything for me. But what relationship can endure being together from a morning shower to an evening soak? Who can feel loving all the time?

I was too young to know the cult of perfection could be fatal. There was no room for me to feel frustrated, angry, or unloving. I was still young and developing my artistic expression while caring for three children. I was trying to learn who I was apart from Paul while he didn't seem to think that was at all important. What mattered was that we were perfectly happy together. Years later I heard a Zen master tell a story about perfection. A monk had been raking a rock garden, working all day, raking over and over, not rushing, but giving complete attention to his work. He didn't want a leaf to be out of place. Still, even though it looked right, he felt something was wrong. He wondered what he had missed even with his thoroughness. The master came along and the monk explained his dilemma. The master looked around, then walked over to a small tree and shook it until a few leaves lay scattered over the raked stones. The monk looked at the garden, smiled, and bowed to his teacher. He realized there can never be perfection without imperfection.

I started sending slides of my work to galleries. One afternoon Paul found me sitting in the kitchen holding a rejection letter for an exhibit. I was deeply disappointed. When I showed it to him he said, "Don't be upset. It doesn't matter. I love your work." I don't know if it was the rejection or his response that plunged me into misery. I sat at the kitchen table sobbing and Paul clearly didn't understand. Together, we enjoyed a lovely home, a full life, and three beautiful children, but he didn't share my personal struggle. He loved my creative spirit and wanted to support it. I was appreciative of his support, but I didn't think he understood my pain. He had his own challenging relationship with the art world. I had yet to learn that rejection is part of the process.

Then I was selected for a two-person show at the Bromfield Gallery in Boston. I would be able to exhibit the complete *Agricultural Tool Series*, fourteen assemblages with poems. Working with these old agricultural tools and old boards I had intuitively related to them. I admired their weather-worn and well-worked patinas. They connected me back to the Japanese aesthetic that had so influenced me. It was with these materials that I could express my distress at the callous destruction of the natural world. Christine Temin, then the *Boston Globe's* art critic, wrote a good review, which buoyed me, but it didn't take long for my feeling of accomplishment to disappear. I wanted to be seen as a professional artist, but when I compared myself with Paul I felt insignificant. He was the Matisse, the raconteur, the one who always had fascinating stories to tell of his lineage and his inventions. Though he would take pleasure and pride in my artwork, I was looking for an acknowledgment from outside. Though he was caring and I loved him, I needed to find something that was my own.

Only much later did I fully grasp that the problem had less to do with what Paul did or didn't do, and everything to do with me and our circumstances. Our age difference was the elephant in the room. I never asked Paul what he thought about marrying a woman so much younger, or if he was worried about our future together. Paul only wanted me to be happy, perhaps believing as long as I was, I would be with him.

No one can make another person happy, no one can complete another person. A natural part of growing up is a journey of self- actualization, and we must make this journey alone. I started working on a second series of sculptures again using old agricultural tools and titled it *Fragments of the Heart*. On a rough-edged board, I attached nails wired flat like elongated drops of rain and gave the piece the title *In Hot Sunlight*.

> sweat droplets
> float seedlike
>
> down brow
> neck and breast
>
> earth is parched
> waiting for rain

In this series I used the old tools to express my longing, loneliness, and frustration. Paul read the poems, but we didn't talk about our relationship. Neither of us talked about our difficulties. We didn't know how to begin.

Paul designed a new bedroom for us with openings for a frieze of cloth panels that would circle the room. We had just come back from a family vacation in Taos, New Mexico. Exhilarated by the mountains, the air, the snow, and the Taos light, I made the panels for our bedroom with the landscape of the southwest, calling them *Southwest Frieze*.

"I won't tolerate them in the room. They have to come down. Please make something that is right."

It was the first time Paul said he didn't like something I made. I had expressed something in my art that he recognized as threatening our relationship. He had sensed I was inhabiting a world he didn't share.

We still didn't talk about these difficulties. Our relationship had become fragile, and we were both terrified. I needed to find something in my life that made me feel independent. I started hiking on Wednesdays in the White Mountains with a group of friends, climbing to the summits of peaks and feeling the thrill of physical challenge. We left at 5:00 a.m., drove three hours north, hiked all day, then returned home. Paul made sure the children had dinner and I got back in time to read them a story before bed. It was the beginning of discovering my own strength. But the more I began to pull away, the more Paul wanted to keep me close. I didn't need him to make it to the top of a mountain—I was on my own. I planned a trip to Colorado with a few friends while the children were in camp. Paul said he would like to go. "No, I'm sorry. It just won't work. These people are really serious hikers. That's all they care about. You wouldn't enjoy it."

"That's all right, I can amuse myself."

"They've already reserved rooms and cars, and arranged the trip."

Paul didn't go on that trip, but when I organized a trek to Nepal with three women friends, he said, "Linda, you can't go to Nepal. If you go our marriage is over." I felt his anger at what I was doing and his fear of losing me. I stayed home while my friends found another woman to take my place.

Our lives continued. I still hiked on Wednesdays, but otherwise worked in my studio, mothered the children, and made sure the household ran smoothly. We had classical music concerts in the "big room," now called the *Kalliroscope Gallery*. We hosted events like the annual **Artists' Valentines**, where over a hundred artists made valentines we sold to raise money for an artist grant.

I made twelve cloth-covered panels that hung in large circle around the room. Each panel had its own colors and simple designs, and written on each one was a word—joy, death, solitude, birth, miracles, judgement, truth, doubt, beauty, jealousy, bliss, and passion. A week after it was installed a friend asked if he could have a memorial service for his mother at our Church. He was the reverend at the Groton Unitarian Church, but wanted a space that was non-ecumenical for his mother's service. A hundred people sat in a circle under the panels sharing memories and singing to ease their loss.

I wrote a four-part poem, "Early Spring," using the names of wildflowers and birds for the composer Harry Chalmiers, a commissioned work for the Montage Chamber Singers. I was exploring new mediums, but Paul and I were growing further apart. We were stuck in old patterns, and my response was to throw myself into making more art. ✾

Row 8: Trobriand Islands, Papua New Guinea

Paul and I were in Paris visiting his mother when my mother's husband, Bill, called to say she was going into the hospital for an operation. The doctor's diagnosis was colon cancer. Immediately, we changed our return flight to fly to New York, arriving at New York University Hospital as she came out of surgery. The surgeon had removed part of her colon and liver. Cancer was in her bloodstream and chemo treatments would follow.

This was shocking news. My mother had become my anchor in the world. Even though we spent little time together, she would always keep in touch, writing letters from wherever she was and calling me from airports while she waited for flights. She had come into her own life during the rise of feminism in the 1970s and was a great advocate and mentor for her female students. She was a strong advocate for me.

In anthropology, it's customary to spend a year doing fieldwork prior to writing one's dissertation, but my mother couldn't stay away from her children and husband for that long. Instead, she arranged to spend May through September doing her fieldwork in the Trobriand Islands

In the Trobriand Islands, Papua New Guinea, 1971

off Papua New Guinea. Then she would return home to family life. The following year she would go back to the field for another five months.

My father supported her and did his best to take care of my brother and me while she was gone. Five months is a long time to be away from one's family. It must have been difficult when he took her to the airport for her international flight. Years later, when he drove me to Kennedy Airport in New York to catch my flight to Japan he asked, "Why can't you just stay home and live nearby?" I later understood my father's inability to appreciate what I was doing. My leaving for Japan was too close to the abandonment he had experienced when my mother left for her fieldwork, and eventually created a different life.

In the annals of anthropology, the Trobriand Islands were made famous by the early twentieth-century British anthropologist Bronislaw Malinowski (1884-1942). His books, *Argonauts of the Western Pacific*, *The Sexual Life of Savages*, and *Coral Gardens and their Magic*, though now dated, established the bar for theoretical debate at the time.

My mother had initially planned to study Trobriand woodcarving, but within days of her arrival the women of the village took her with them to a *sagali*, a mortuary ceremony, in a neighboring village. She described a *sagali* in her first book, *Women of Value, Men of Renown: New Perspectives in Trobriand Exchange*. Hundreds of people gathered, mostly women, with large baskets of *doba*, "money" made from banana leaf bundles, along with grass skirts, pieces of calico cloth, baskets of yams, and even Australian dollars—at that time, Papua New Guinea was a territory of Australia. The *sagali* was a ceremony to pay back the mourners of a man who had died a year ago. Death creates a hole in the fabric of a society. In the Trobriands, people mourn for at least a year, sometimes longer, following different practices. Some people blacken their faces, while others blacken their entire bodies. One person will carry the deceased's straw bag in which he would have carried his mustard, betel nut, and lime stick. Others will prepare special foods for the deceased's family. The *sagali* is the ritual to repay these people for their mourning. It's a way to restitch the torn fabric of the society.

Malinowski, in his three volumes about the Trobriand Islands, never mentioned a *sagali*. These bare-breasted women and their complicated exchanges either didn't interest him, or he felt incapable of becoming close enough with them to get information. It was the Trobriand men he wrote about. Malinowski described their extensive trade routes in dugout canoes to exchange valuable shells throughout the South Pacific, an impressive way for men to grow their fame. He completely missed the importance of women. My mother discovered that the women controlled the family wealth, and this wealth gave them tremendous power.

When my mother returned from the Trobriands, she was a changed person. She no longer felt defined by her parents, marriage, or children. She asked my younger brother, Jon, and me to call her "Anna" instead of "Mom." This name change was linked to the new person she had become upon beginning fieldwork.

I learned that the suggestion for this change came from anthropologist Ann Chowning. Anna met Ann in Port Moresby, the capital of Papua New Guinea, where she landed to gather supplies before flying to the Trobriands. Over dinner they had discussed my mother's fieldwork and Ann had asked what she planned to call herself in the field. In my mother's field diary she had written:

> I told her that I had never thought of anything but
> "Annette." Ann [Chowning] was far more
> sophisticated linguistically about the Trobriands
> than I, and thought "Annette" would not be a
> propitious sound within the Kiriwina language.
> I decided at dinner that I would call myself "Anna."
> Annette means "little Ann," and I did not feel so
> "little" anymore, Anna better suited my new persona.

The following spring, when Anna was making plans to return to New Guinea, she asked me and my brother if we wanted to go with her. Jon chose to stay home with our father, but I said I wanted to go. I was fifteen.

On the first morning in the village, roosters and *sakau* birds woke us. I accompanied the village women to a cave over a rocky trail to get fresh water. On our second night in the village I remember hearing long, low keening, then a tap-tap on our banana leaf door. "Come! Come!" Our elderly neighbor had died, and his wife and children were grieving. We entered the low doorway of a small hut. A kerosene light lit the scene. The small room was packed with villagers sitting on the floor. We squeezed in. The deceased man was laid out over the legs of his family, naked except for a pandanas-leaf loincloth. Women were painting designs in deep blood red all over his body using a mixture of betel nut juice (the betel nut is from the areca palm tree and hallucinogenic when chewed in quantity), lime, and mustard to decorate his sleep. Uncontrollable crying came over the group, and then the voices settled down to whispers. Occasionally someone said something funny and laughter erupted, then the room quieted until weeping took over again. This vigil lasted throughout the night. The man's grave was dug early the next day and he was buried that afternoon. Our neighbors started their long vigil of blackening their faces and bodies, a sign they were in mourning. The rest of the village resumed its normal activities.

On some days we followed a villager into the garden, on other days we stayed in the hamlet and watched as women cooked or wove grass skirts. Most days nothing special happened, only the clamor and silence of village life. Occasionally I went with some young people to sit by the road. I wasn't sure if we were looking for a ride to the main town or just sitting there. I always wore a string around my neck and took it out to make string figures. In this way I interacted with the whole village, young as well as old, playing cat's cradle even though I could only speak a few words of their language.

Once some children approached me, shaking live grasshoppers and shouting, *Kukwamu! Kukwamu!* [Eat it.] And I did, crunching and swallowing quickly. I was under strict instructions to not become involved with any young people. Anna didn't want any complications in her relationships with the islanders stemming from romantic involvements on my part.

The shock of Anna's diagnosis prompted her to begin writing a memoir. Its focus was how living in the Trobriand Islands had changed the course of her life. Though she had published three academic books, she wanted to share her personal journey. The first chapter begins in her office at New York University, where she is reading a letter from a friend in New Guinea about Lepani Watson, a renowned Trobriander.

Lepani had been diagnosed with colon cancer while living in Port Moresby, but had asked to be taken back to the Trobriand Islands so he might die in the house where he was born. For three days and nights, refusing any food or water, Lepani sat on a mat in the middle of his house, often alone. He chanted his Trobriand knowledge—what he knew about shell exchanges, canoe sailing, and land rights; magic spells for the growing of yam gardens, canoe sailing, love magic; stories of adultery, old disputes, and sorcery. He said it was necessary for him to lighten his body by releasing what he knew. Then he lay back on his mat and died.

Hearing Lepani's story empowered Anna to reflect on her life and to face her cancer diagnosis with purpose and strength. She wrote over a hundred pages, but as the disease progressed, she became too weak to finish the manuscript. She confided in me how disappointed she was to leave this project unfinished. Without thinking I said, "I'll finish it for you." On one of our visits to her husband Bill's farmhouse in Vermont, Anna sent me to the small room over the garage where she had created a studio of her own.

"There are two cardboard boxes. One is marked 'Letters from the field' and the other 'Personal letters.'"

I found the boxes and loaded them into my car.

Anna lived bravely with her illness, dying three years after her diagnosis. She left no instructions for her ashes. When I thought about where they might be spread, the Trobriands were the only place that seemed right. After all, she had written in her memoir, "If the Trobriands were once the source of my rebirth, then it is only fitting that my death be moored to these anthropologically sacred islands in an equally intimate way." When I mentioned this to Bill, he agreed, but he had no interest in making the trip. He had done extensive fieldwork in the Sepik area of New Guinea and been to the Trobriands with Anna on two later trips. He didn't want to go back. When I told Anna's brother, Bob, I wanted to go, he said, "That's what I thought you would do."

Three months after Anna's death, I left for the Trobriand Islands. I hadn't been on a trip by myself since I left Japan and moved in with Paul. I had never even gone down to New York on my own "to take a class" as Anna had hoped. When I told Paul I would take my mother's ashes back to the Trobriand Islands, our children were nine, eleven, and fourteen.

"I'll go with you," he immediately said. "We can do this together."

After a short hesitation I answered, "I need to do this myself."

"I'd like to go with you, Linda."

"I want to do this myself," I said.

I made arrangements to be away for three weeks. When Paul dropped me off at Logan Airport in Boston, I had two pieces of luggage: a duffle bag to check and a red carry-on knapsack I had borrowed from Nick. Tucked in the bottom of the knapsack was the canister with Anna's ashes, wrapped in a black-and-white leaf-patterned scarf. In the days before preflight screening, the metal can I carried was not detected.

Before landing in the Trobriand Islands, I visited the Highlands and stopped at several Sepik River villages on the mainland. Bill had given me a pocketknife, a gift for one of his old friends. When the boat stopped near the village where he had done fieldwork, I gave the knife to someone who promised to deliver it. I had also brought a small computer with me to stay in touch with Paul, but once I was there it was the last thing I wanted to do. I felt such elation at being free, being on my own. I took everything in—people, colors, sensations—without Paul's filter. The contrast was startling. I hadn't realized how much I had depended on him and his views of the world. I met the strong Highland women who carried over one hundred pounds of potatoes on their backs using a trumpline around their foreheads. I visited the village of the Huli Wigmen, where men grew out their hair and then cut it to fashion large geometrically-shaped wigs for ritual dances. I set out by boat to travel from the New Guinea mainland to the Trobriand Islands. Along the way, I went scuba diving along a pristine reef with a fellow traveler. We did a series of drift dives, passing by twenty-foot-high coral fans and through schools of vibrantly colored fish. We were diving through waters known only to fish and eels.

I knew it would be complicated to take Anna's ashes back to the village. *Where exactly would they be spread? Who would own the land? How much would I have to pay?* I decided it was better to release them into the water. The night before the boat docked in the Trobriands, one of the crew on the boat rowed me out in a rubber Zodiac to a place between Kiriwina, the largest of the Trobriand Islands, the one where Anna had done her fieldwork, and Tuma, an uninhabited island where the Trobrianders believe spirits of the dead go and from where children come. Being gently rocked by the waves, under billows of clouds brightly lit by a three-quarter moon, I said goodbye, thanking her for the gift of life. I already missed her. I flung her ashes into the darkness—the wind blew them back into my face.

The next morning, when we docked in the small town of Losuia on Kiriwina, I found a driver with a truck to take me the seven miles to the entrance of Kwaibwaga, our village. I had written to the villagers in advance and they were expecting me. At the sound of the truck's motor, they rushed out to the road. To my surprise, beginning with the chief, they each held me in a strong embrace and wept, mourning our mutual loss. It had been twenty-seven years since I had been there, but they knew about mourning, about rituals, about the rift in a society when someone dies.

The village had changed. I saw fewer young people. It felt poor, almost forgotten, as if the life force was missing. And indeed, it was missing. With the changes brought by western influences, many of the children had left for the capital and elsewhere in search of a different life. They didn't want to be slash-and-burn farmers, perpetually poor, dressed in traditional grass skirts or loincloths or some hand-me-down calico piece of clothing. The young people had been to school and wanted western dress, watches, and trade-store food. They wanted lives outside the confines of village life, with skills and professions to join the larger world.

I brought gifts of rice, betel nut, and a stack of old black-and-white photos I had taken when I lived there. Everyone was desperate for whatever they could get, and I felt the tension over who should distribute these gifts. Bomapota, the woman who had been Anna's household helper when she lived there, took the bag of rice. I walked around the village and distributed the betel nut to the older women in Anna's honor. These were the women Anna had gotten to know, who had taught her about life from their perspective. Now skinny, often toothless and with flat, droopy breasts, they smiled broadly when I offered them the betel nut.

In my mother's memoir she wrote about the surprising way she became "known" to the village women. Before flying to the Trobriands, in addition to meeting with Ann Chowning, she met an Australian filmmaker, Kyle. He was wrapping up the filming for a BBC program with David Attenborough about some tribes living in the New Guinea Highlands. Kyle had been intrigued by this attractive woman in her forties, a mother, about to begin fieldwork alone in the famous Trobriand Island atolls. They shared a few beers, and then Kyle returned to Australia and Anna finished her preparations for the Trobriands. They exchanged letters over the next month until Kyle said he was returning to Papua New Guinea to shoot some more footage. Anna wrote in her diary:

> I struggled with my conscience, but asked if he might
> detour his trip a few days and visit me. I was overjoyed
> when he wrote he would arrive in two weeks on the
> Saturday morning flight.

Then the big question was how to introduce him to the villagers. By then she knew enough about Trobriand kinship taboos not to introduce him as her brother or her father's brother. But if he was her mother's brother, then he could properly stay in her hut.

Kyle had packed the ingredients for a magnificent field dinner: two steaks on dry ice, a superb bottle of Australian cabernet sauvignon, and giant glazed apricots for dessert. She wrote, ". . . and by the time the cocks crowed right before daybreak, I was unabashedly in love."

After Kyle left, Anna wanted to hide away in her hut. The contrast of primitive life after three days with Kyle was another kind of culture shock. She wrote:

> I shut my door—something I never did in the middle
> of the afternoon . . . . In half an hour I heard that familiar
> scratching on my palm frond wall and my response was
> anger at the inability of people to leave me alone . . . .
> "Anna, your food. Not more than than five minutes
> passed, when the same situation arose with Ruth,
> Bomapota's mother. This was only the beginning as
> a whole parade of women, ten of them in total
> brought me food. I never received so many plates
> of food in the same day, and I wondered why so many
> women, all at the same time, suddenly were so generous.
> Then a half an hour later, Bomapota came into the
> house and said, "Quickly, you must get up. The women
> are gathered in front of your house and
> want to talk to you."

Anna was grumpy, but went outside on the verandah. One of the women said to her, "Anna, he was not your mother's brother." She stuck to her story until one woman finally shifted the conversation.

"Are you sad?" she asked.

With this question, Anna's relationship with the Trobriand women changed. They knew, and Anna knew they knew—Kyle was her lover and she was sad at his departure. Their empathy was unforgettable. Sharing this poignant experience with these women broke through every cultural barrier that previously existed.

I distributed the photographs to those people who recognized villagers in them—a son, a cousin, or a mother. One photo was of a small naked boy holding a sardine can to his ear. A woman quickly put her hand over it. "That is her brother," she said, pointing to a woman near us. "She should not see him naked."

Later in the afternoon, I took the truck back to Losuia and boarded the boat to begin the long journey back home. Like my mother after her first field trip, when I returned, I was changed. Paul knew it. I remember tapping a drumbeat, and he said, "Don't do that." I went through the motions of resuming our shared life, but some tether had been cut. Once again, we didn't talk about it; we simply picked up our lives. But it was as if Anna had sent me on this trip knowing exactly what I needed. She had missed the school plays and making home-baked cookies, but in the end it didn't matter. She was there when it counted most. She loved Paul and her grandchildren; she knew from her own divorce the trauma of breaking up a family. But she also knew I needed to discover my place in the world. I needed the opportunity to grow away from the shade cast by Paul.

The trip to the Tobriand Islands with Anna's ashes was my wake-up call, but I couldn't imagine breaking up our family. I decided I would stay in the marriage and make the best of it until the children were older. But increasingly unhappy, I knew I was no good for Paul, for our children, or for myself.

We were still in bed, the sun streaming in the Palladian window, surrounded by the beige, white, and rose-colored cloth panel frieze, the second set I made for our room. Looking at one of the panels with the words blossoms—morning—dew, I said, "Paul, I can't do this anymore."

He understood. He simply said, "You'll have to find a new place to live."

When I think back to that morning, to that decision, my heart tightens. Breaking up my marriage of almost twenty years was the hardest thing I have ever done. To our children, the news came without warning, a simple conversation around the kitchen table. "Your mother is leaving me," Paul said. "We're getting divorced." I remember the disbelief on their young faces. I remember the sickening feeling of wanting my body, my entire being, to sink into oblivion. I can't remember reaching out to them, to hold them, to touch them, because of my own mortification. Their father's words severed our connection. Paul presented the divorce as a unilateral decision he had had nothing to do with.

Alex was seventeen, Nick fourteen, and Ariel twelve. They left the kitchen and went upstairs to their rooms. Did they talk about it to each other? Or did they suffer silently and alone? I don't know. I never asked. It was too painful, and I was too scared. Too lost myself, I didn't know how to help them. I couldn't talk about their pain, when I had no words to describe my own. I didn't know what I was doing, why, or how the unraveling of our marriage had begun. I could go back in my mind to that seed planted by Nam June Paik, to my mother's concerns, to the difference in our ages, but I didn't want to erase all the love Paul and I had shared.

For most of our friends the news arrived as a complete shock. Paul showed me the note he sent everyone on his email list saying, Linda is leaving me. It was the truth, but the reality, as it always is, was more complex. Paul would keep the church and the art he had inherited from his parents, and I would move out. The children would be free to go between our two houses, the church and the farm—now my new home.

Naming the farm *Old Frog Pond Farm* connected me to Japan, the Noh theater, and Zen poets; to the exquisite gardens, to the beauty and sadness that are inextricably bound in the traditional Japanese world. The name took me back to the time when I was young, single, and had plunged into the world of traditional Japan. Once again, I was starting a new life. I had a farm and an orchard, and despite the naysayers saying, "It's hard to grow apples!" I was going to do my best to grow a crop of organic apples. ❋

The Art of Growing

The pruning process begins early in the life of the tree, and continues ceaselessly until the end. To the apple-tree in the wind, strict pruning is the assurance of success. No tree can reach maturity unless more parts perish than are able to live.

—Liberty Hyde Bailey

Row 9: Pick Your Own

Organic certification was a priority. When I looked online at the list of certified local farms, I discovered there were no pick-your-own certified organic orchards in Massachusetts—our farm would be the first. *Yes,* becoming certified would create the market. If the farm attracted enough people to pick apples, then I wouldn't need to be picking, marketing, and transporting—all of which I hadn't really considered, but which would be necessary if people didn't pick their own.

Today, *organic* is an adjective firmly planted in the popular domain. In stores we find organic cotton, organic raisins, organic sunscreen. The use of "organic" on the label is the selling point, and thus we even have organic wild rice and organic salmon. When I decided to bring the orchard back to life and do it organically, the term was not used as often. I didn't follow an organic lifestyle. I wasn't a diehard foodie or a fanatic macrobiotic follower. I cooked from scratch, avoiding mixes and prepared foods, but my habits were formed from an inclination to eat simply. I liked fresh food. I knew organic would sell our apples, but for this first year I wouldn't advertise since even with Denis's help,

Schoolchildren visit the orchard, 2007

I couldn't know for sure we would have a crop. I decided to rely on the combination of Frank Carlson buying our organic apples and on roadside signs.

How does one become certified to grow organic apples? Who awards this revered and valuable designation? When a farmer wants to be an organic grower and label his or her produce accordingly, each crop on the farm must be certified annually. The United States Department of Agriculture (USDA), through the National Organic Program (NOP), approves local certifying organizations. Here in southern New England, Baystate Organic Certifiers is our accrediting agent.

First, the rules require a farm demonstrate for three years the land has been free from contaminating chemicals. That requirement was easy since I could prove our orchard hadn't had chemicals applied to it for the five years before I bought it and it had been three years since I took over its care. Second, the crops must be grown *according* to organic standards. Specifically, every material used must be on the Organic Materials Review Institute's (OMRI) list or individually approved by a certifying agency. If a farmer chooses not to become certified yet still follows all of the regulations, he or she can tell customers the crop is grown according to organic standards but cannot label it organic. The standards are stringent, and the USDA can slap a fine of up to $17,000 for each infraction. (Growers who bring in less than $5,000 a year are exempt.) I was determined to grow our apples organically whether or not we were certified, but I needed certification to advertise and attract customers.

I submitted thirty pages of paperwork to Baystate Certifiers, including maps of the land, a soil report, harvest procedures, selling and storage plans, a list of materials I planned to use for pest management, disease management, and weed management. In addition, I answered questions about compost, manure, irrigation, and abutters. The certifying agency wanted to be sure there was no possibility of contamination at any step in the process of delivering the crop to the consumer. The final requirement before receiving certification was an onsite inspection. This would be scheduled in the next couple of months. I told myself not to worry.

Meanwhile, I learned about a group of New England apple growers who gathered once a year to talk about apples. They called themselves the *Holistic Apple Growers* and their meeting was scheduled for the first week in March, in three weeks. I asked Denis if he wanted to come with me. We arrived at a small retreat center in Hawley, Massachusetts, in time for a hearty lunch. In the dining room, an earthy energy emanated from the thirty or so rugged men in Carharts, flannel shirts, and work boots. There was only one other woman there. A thin man with a long gray beard had Felco clippers hanging on his belt, just in case something needed pruning.

The first apple-growing session began in the large upstairs room of the barn. The woodstove was fired up, and an odd assortment of chairs and sofas made a large circle. The organizer, Michael Phillips, a bearded, Santa Claus-like man, cleared his throat. "Let's go around the room and introduce our orchards."

The man on Michael's right with the pruners on his belt was Bill MacKentley from Potsdam, New York. The owner of St. Lawrence Nurseries, he specialized in fruit trees for northern climates. The other female in the group was a young woman who worked at his nursery. Bill seemed incredibly knowledgeable, quick, and opinionated. Certainly cold-hardy himself, he later said, "Ah, we start planting trees when there are still a couple inches of frost in the ground."

John Bunker spoke next. He ran Fedco Trees in Maine and organized the growing and selling of thousands of fruit trees every year. He had his own orchard at his house in Palermo, and was passionate about Maine's heirloom varieties. Brian Caldwell, a grower in New York, was an organic vegetable researcher at Cornell University. He had two small orchards near his home. I was starting to feel intimidated as my turn approached.

"I recently moved to a farm with an abandoned apple orchard," I said, "and I am trying to bring it back using only organic materials.

But I'm a sculptor, and I don't know anything about apples, but Denis does," gesturing to him. "He's helping me."

Everyone seemed very polite; no one hinted I was in over my head, or embarking on something impossible.

"How many trees do you have?" asked a handsome man with an Australian accent.

"I have about two hundred. I had to remove one hundred dead trees."

"Do you know the varieties?" John Bunker asked.

"Red Delicious, Golden Delicious, Blushing Golden, Macoun, and McIntosh," I said, "but we're going to plant some heirlooms and new disease-resistant varieties."

"How many Red Delicious do you have?" John asked.

"We have about fifty," Denis answered for me.

He then went on to say, "I used to manage a conventional orchard—Nashoba Winery. I'd like to hear about the different organic materials we can use in Linda's orchard."

Denis and I heard about Permaculture and Biodynamics, about the organic pesticide Entrust and the organic fungicide Serenade. I scribbled down these endearing names. Liberty, Freedom, Dayton, and Enterprise were suggested as scab-resistant apple varieties for me to plant. *Did they really think Dayton or Enterprise sounded appetizing?*

One grower said he still used two sprays of Imaden, a chemical pesticide, to make sure he had a clean crop. There was no judgment. Wherever the orchardist fell on the spectrum—certified organic; organic but not certified; mostly organic; or self-described as sustainable, holistic, or naturally grown—the emphasis was on sharing information and ideas so we could each do our best for our orchards' health.

Hugh Williams, the rugged Australian, said he had been growing apples for forty years, adding coyly, "I'm waiting for the day I can be rid of my sprayer."

Alan Suprenant told us about a biodynamic technique called "peppering" to get rid of a particular pest. To use this approach properly, you needed to capture a good number of the pests, burn them, then distribute the ash around the perimeter of the area you wanted to protect. He did this when he had a terrible rat problem in his chicken coop. He added, "You don't cover the entire perimeter, but leave an opening for the rats to leave." He swore it took care of his rat problem for good, and he wondered if we could use this technique for the plum curculio. The challenge, everyone agreed, was in gathering enough beetles to make the ash.

Another grower, Scott Bolotin, told us about an apple tree he had grafted with 250 different kinds of apples. He passed around his notebook with an indecipherable sketch of names and branches. When I looked quizzically at Denis, he said, "I'll show you how to do that."

I took notes on everything that was said. *Plant disease-resistant trees. Spray Surround for plum curculio. Use mating disruption for codling moth. Feed the soil. Get rid of sprayer, someday.* It all sounded good to me. I had found people who were already doing what I was just beginning to articulate. I would bring the orchard back to fruitful production without harming the earth or its creatures. Although the group offered neither an exact formula nor a guarantee of success, I was excited. I was part of a discussion about growing fruit that was nourishing to the soil and our bodies. Even though we wouldn't see each other until the following year, this "applehood" was supportive. Denis and I returned home armed with new ideas and a copy of Michael's book, *The Holistic Apple Grower*. Denis was skeptical about some of what we had heard. He doubted whether kaolin clay would keep away the nasty plum curculios and wondered what we would do for codling moth, but I was enthusiastic, innocent about the realities of apple pests.

Before I left the meeting, John Bunker walked over and said, "I visit Concord quite often. I could stop by and show you how to change some of your Red Delicious trees to other varieties. Red Delicious, while once a delicious and popular apple, no longer has the same appeal. He told me he would visit mid-May, after blossom, when the trees would be at their most productive, the optimal time to graft. I was thrilled. He was so friendly and clearly in love with everything apples. I later learned he's known as the "apple whisperer" for his work to rediscover the lost apples of Maine. He's always getting boxes of apples in the mail from people who have an unidentified tree on their property and want to know its name. ❧

Row 10: Pollination

Denis reminded me we would need bees for pollination. I found the name of a beekeeper through the Worcester County Beekeepers Association and called Gus Skamarycz. A past president of the association, Gus was eighty-four. He had been keeping honeybees for over fifty years. I told him we were in the process of getting our organic certification. For a small fee, he said, he would bring his bees because he knew we wouldn't spray anything harmful. He said to call him when the buds were at *pink*.

Orchardists have their own terms to define the journey from bud to fruit. *Dormant* describes the trees in winter, when the buds are gray-brown and tightly closed. The trees appear lifeless, but their metabolic activity is simply very low. They are waiting for the right combination of temperature and length of daylight to awaken. The outer sheath on the bud is a winter quilt protecting the folded blossom inside. Once the apple bud breaks dormancy, the fruit bud scales at the tip separate and reveal light gray tissue. This stage is called *silver tip*.

The next stage is *green tip*. The buds, in response to warmth and

Our first beekeeper and his hives, 2007

light, begin to plump. The tip opens further to reveal a green fuzz, the first sight of living plant tissue. The next stage, *half-inch green* or *mouse ears*, is an apt description as two tiny oblong leaves appear.

Tight cluster follows with a rosette of green leaves around a tightly packed flower bud. *Pink* stage is next, as this singular flower bud separates into six individual pink-sheathed blossom buds. This is the most exciting moment in the orchard, for each of these flower buds, if pollinated, will become an apple. In the center the *king blossom* opens first. It's the strongest and largest bud. The others follow; reserves for the tree in case something happens to the *king. Full bloom* is when all blossoms are open. Pollinators arrive from far and wide to drink sweet apple nectar and in the case of honeybees, bring it back to their hives.

On May 6, I called Gus about the bees. The trees had reached pink, and the buds would soon open. He arrived before sunup with two hives, and I walked with him into the quiet orchard. His bees were asleep.

"Why so early?" I asked.

"I want the bees to open their eyes in a new place, see the blossoms, and go to work." He told me if he moved them to a new location when the flowers were not yet in bloom, they might venture far afield seeking food and perhaps not return to the hive. Bees can easily become disoriented and not know where they are, even if a hive is moved only a few feet.

"How long does it take a hive to pollinate an orchard?" I asked.

Looking around, Gus said, "A strong hive can pollinate this orchard in a few hours, but you have different varieties."

He was right. Not all of our trees bloom at the same time. The McIntosh apples open first; the Golden Blushing reach blossom a full two weeks later. The Cortland and the Golden Delicious are in between. Gus's bees would stay for two weeks to ensure pollination of all the trees.

Gus told me Albert Einstein said, "If the bee disappeared off the face of the earth, man would only have four years left to live."

"What do you think is the cause of today's decline?" I asked.

"It's the Imidacloprid," Gus blurted out. "I've been telling people for twenty years, and no one will listen."

Imidacloprid is one of the neonicotinoids, the family of insecticides linked to the drastic death of many bee populations. It's toxic not only to bees, but also to earthworms, fish, and amphibians when it leaches into groundwater. Many European countries have banned its use, yet it remains readily available in the United States. It's one of the most widely used pesticides in the world.

"I can't believe it's not banned everywhere," I said.

Gus replied, "The corporations do the testing."

I later found out Imdacloprid is one of the chemicals that generates the most profit for its producers; companies take the position they can't afford to stop making it.

Trillions of pounds of toxic chemicals are still spread over our limited topsoil and sprayed into air and water causing the deaths of insects, amphibians, birds, plants, and humans. Companies use their profits to pay lobbyists. Bureaucracy works at a turtle's pace to pass new regulations. And when the people in power prefer money in their pocket to the health of the planet, the result is devastating.

Villagers who live on the border between Nepal and China must hand pollinate their apple trees because their bees have disappeared. These farmers gather, dry, and grind pollen which they put in small boxes and wear around their necks. Using a cigarette filter or a pencil eraser, they touch the pollen and then the sticky, pillow-like stigmas in the center of the blossoms to hand-pollinate each bud. I couldn't imagine hand-pollinating our entire orchard.

I love watching the bees reach down inside the apple blossom to suck up sweet ambrosia. As the bee dives, it brushes against the anthers of the flower and grains of pollen stick like Velcro to its body hairs. It spreads these pollen grains from flower to flower. A single bee will visit fifty to a hundred trees in an outing. It then carries the nectar back to the hive and heads out again, visiting over 2000 flowers in one day.

Different species have different pollination practices. However, most plants, like most apples, require cross-pollination to ensure genetic diversity. In scientific terms this process is referred to as self-incompatible. These plants all need another plant in their life cycle to bear fruit. I liked this notion of needing others. I was certainly grateful for the community of people I was meeting who were sharing their knowledge and experience with apples.

When I walked through the orchard I felt the vibration of buzzing all over my body. I would often stop and watch a single bee. Its furry rump up in the air, a back leg delicately perched on the edge of a flower, its head stretching deep down into the blossom. Then it would pop up and fly off to the next flower. No hesitation. No indecision about where to go amidst so many choices.

Two weeks later Gus arrived to pick up his bees.

"Where do you take them?" I asked.

They go to the brothers, a monastery in southern New Hampshire. "Bears are a problem in their area," he told me. The monks put the hives inside a small shed. On the outside wall they cut a narrow slot so the bees can fly from the safety of their hive into the orchard. A long row of sharp nails on the outside of the shed prevents bears from clawing their way inside. ❧

Row 11: A Fungus Among Us

A few weeks later, Denis called with another assignment: "Linda, you're going to need a sprayer. You'll have to spray the trees if you want fruit. I've done some research and have some suggestions for organic sprays."

With the decision to grow apples organically, I had dropped the standard arsenal, but Denis knew we would have to substitute organic materials for chemical pesticides if we wanted a crop. The diseases and pests were lining up.

The Spauldings had sold their sprayer. "Give a call to Oesco, the orchard equipment company in Conway, Massachusetts. Sometimes they have used sprayers," Denis suggested.

I first called Billie Rosenberger. I knew she and her husband had closed Hillbrook Orchards, the orchard in Groton where the children and I used to pick apples. I imagined they might have a sprayer in their barn. Maybe she would sell it to me. Billie was reticent. I suspected she still hoped to use it again on their hillside of apple trees. I called Oesco as Denis had suggested, and they had a used Rears airblast

Spraying sulfur in the orchard

sprayer for sale.

Denis and Caleb were at the farm the day our sprayer arrived. An enormous, orange, 300-gallon cylindrical tank on wheels was lowered from a flatbed trailer. Walking around it, I marveled as if a jet airplane had been delivered. When pulled behind the tractor, attached to the power takeoff, an airblast sprayer delivers a fine mist that coats all the leaves and fruit. Denis did the calculations and calibrations so we'd know exactly how much material to deliver to our two acres of trees, the engine RPM, and the speed of travel down the orchard rows.

His first concern was apple scab fungus, *Venturia inaequalis*, one of the early apple diseases and one of the worst problems for organic orchardists in New England. Denis advised I spray micronized sulfur to combat the scab fungus. Sulfur, a common material used in agriculture to fight fungal infections, is permitted under organic regulations. The Sumerians of ancient Mesopotamia used sulfur 4500 years ago to combat fungal disease in their crops. If it worked in the cradle of civilization, it should work here. He also suggested I buy five gallons of lime sulfur, a more potent material, but also organic.

Scab fungus overwinters on the orchard floor. In the early spring, after a warm, rainy period, millions of spores float upward like dust motes in sunlight. Landing on the new green leaves, warm and wet, the scab first shows up as innocuous looking smoky spots, but gradually these cloudy patches grow darker and spread over the leaf surface. Unchecked, the fungus becomes rampant and jumps from leaf to developing fruit. The apples develop brown crusty scabs, grow misshapen, and eventually crack. That's what I had seen last summer when I walked through the orchard. Brown leaves and barely any fruit. I knew for a fact this scourge of the New England apple thrived in our orchard.

Denis showed Caleb how to hook up the sprayer, and the first spray of the apple season went into the tank—four pounds of copper to prevent fire blight, a bacterium that spreads from flower to flower carried by bees at blossom time which will systemically kill a tree, and twenty pounds of sulfur for scab, all mixed in 300 gallons of water. Suited up in white Tyvek one-piece hooded overalls, green rubber gloves, facemask, and goggles, Caleb looked like a spaceman. He headed into the orchard. Bon voyage. The whir of the tractor and the misty spray cloud drifted through the sky on that quiet spring day.

Denis turned to me. "Linda," he said, in the matter-of-fact tone I had come to recognize as meaning *something else is needed.* "You're going to have to renew the sulfur after any period of rain for the next six weeks if it has been over five days since the last spray."

I was flabbergasted.

"Spray that many times for scab?" I asked. Denis nodded.

From my reading I knew sulfur wasn't a surefire prevention; at best it was moderately effective. Conventional orchards use an array of chemical fungicides throughout the season. We were only changing the pH of the leaves to make it inhospitable for the scab spores to take purchase and grow.

With so many sulfur sprays required, I knew I would also be spraying. I was nervous driving the tractor and pulling the fifteen-foot sprayer. In tight places it's challenging to back up with the sprayer attached. *What if I hit a tree turning into the next row?* Caleb helped me the first time. He walked in front of the tractor like a drum major leading a parade. He had to gesture with exaggerated motions since we were both wearing ear protection. He showed me how far I needed to swing out at the end of each row. Some turns were easy, but others had almost no clearance. Caleb waved his arms frantically: *Turn here! Turn here!* He didn't want me to hit my neighbor Ed's stone wall.

Meanwhile, mastery of the controls was essential. A small lever for the left set of sprayer nozzles, another for the right, and a third in the center turned them on and off. If I didn't manage to turn off one side in time, I sprayed my face as I angled into the next row. When passing a place where a tree was missing in the row, I needed to be alert and turn off those nozzles, then turn them back on before reaching the next tree. I didn't want to waste the spray.

Caleb and I had long conversations. He always wanted me to spray more often to be sure the trees were protected. My instinct was to spray less. I worried too much sulfur would adversely affect the trees. There was no clear protocol providing certainty. It might rain or it might not. Should I spray before a sixty percent chance of rain, or with a forty percent chance? If I waited till the rain started, it was too late.

I didn't want to bother Denis who was working on his landscape properties and who also wasn't billing me for anything except our pruning days together. He had instructed me on the general guidelines of what to do, and it was now up to me to find my way. I'd talk with Caleb, but the decision was mine.

When I decided it was a day to spray, I filled the tank with 250 gallons of water, turned on the power takeoff, and checked the nozzles. Usually some of them were clogged with grit picked up from the spray materials. I removed each spray unit and unclogged the perforated discs that control the spray density. I learned to always keep a few paper clips attached to the tractor.

After these preliminaries, I suited up, and gathered my respirator, ear muffs, sunglasses, and rubber gloves. Then I turned on the power takeoff again to run the tank agitator while pouring the spray materials into the whirling water. Up and down lifting five-gallon buckets of measured liquids or heavy bags of powders that needed to be slowly poured into the tank, I was never sure I was doing the right thing. Sometimes I changed the percentages at the last minute, or added something else.

Once I was finally on the tractor and lined up at the start of the first row, I shifted into slow mode, set the RPMs at 1700, put the gear stick into third, released the clutch, and turned on the nozzles. Turtle pace became the new normal, and it hardly seemed I had time to study the tree when it had already passed me by. I wanted to see everything: the leaves, the buds, a broken branch, a bird's nest, insect damage, a butterfly, a dense clutch of black bugs. However, I had to be awake or *whack!* A branch would snap back and hit me in the face.

I found I liked observing the trees from the height and proximity of the tractor seat. Looking backwards, I would check on the spray, making sure it was coming out evenly on both sides. The patterns of droplets fanned skyward in the sunlight and then fell like an enormous sea fan, an exuberant expression of water that attracted blue and green dragonflies.

If any spray was left over when I reached the last row, I put the tractor into one gear higher and wove my way back until the tank was empty. With the spraying complete, I turned off the power takeoff, lowered the RPMs, and drove back to the chicken coop, the loud whirring now silent. I peeled off rubber gloves, sunglasses, breathing mask, hood, and earmuffs, and stripped off my Tyvek suit. The last step was to power-rinse the tractor, then go inside for a shower.

Spraying had taken several hours during which I was totally concentrated on every tree. It's shape, health, age, and branch structure, and inhabitants. The orchard and I were developing a relationship. However, I would spend the rest of the day doing something that didn't require me to be bumping up and down on the tractor. ❋

Row 12: Cross-Inspection, Cross-Pollination

On the day of our appointment, the inspector arrived with copies of our application and a clipboard of questions. He wanted to see the shed where we stored the sprayer and other tools, our spray log, our storage cabinet for the materials we were using, receipts for all purchases—in short, everything related to the farm operation. It was a bit like having a nosy neighbor peering into every corner and interrogating about pesky details, scribbling notes all the while.

I thought I'd done everything correctly.

"Linda," the inspector said, "I have a note here to check on your copper."

"What?" This was news to me.

I opened the metal cabinet and pulled out the bag of copper.

"Copper sulfate, copper oxychloride, and inert ingredients," he read. "The first two are fine, but you're going to have to find out about the inert ingredients."

The package, from a large and well-established national company, said "Copper" in bold letters. Copper is a mined material, an elemental

With Blase Provitola at the farm

mineral; I never imagined it wasn't organic. I hadn't thought about the inert ingredients and neither had Denis.

"What do I do?" I asked our inspector.

"You'll have to call the company and get them to identify the inert ingredients in writing," he said. "Otherwise you might be ineligible for another three years."

Big companies don't necessarily want to reveal their ingredients. This seemingly small snag could be a serious setback. I put in a call to the company as soon as the inspector left. Someone would return my call.

A few days later, John Bunker arrived from Maine with three varieties of apples he thought I'd enjoy having in our orchard: Jonafree, a recently developed red apple with some immunity to apple scab; Wickson, a crabapple-size fruit with a sharp, but sweet taste; and Williams Pride, a delicious new early-season apple. He transported these new varieties as scion wood—thin, twelve-inch twigs of healthy, first-year growth cut from his trees sometime in February, wrapped in plastic to keep in moisture, and stored in the fridge until now. We wouldn't be creating "a tree of many colors" like the apple grower with 250 varieties on one tree, but with John's scion wood, we would change three rows of our Red Delicious trees to new varieties, using a technique called "topworking."

I had invited Denis to join us. The three of us faced the first large Red Delicious tree. Without hesitating, Denis pulled the cord of his chain saw and sawed off the trunk four feet above the ground. I stood back in awe—almost the entire tree was decapitated. Denis had left one large lower lateral branch. John responded to my look of uncertainty.

"You leave a good-sized branch or two on the trunk to keep the tree alive and feed the roots while your grafts are small."

Denis "topped" the rest of the trees in the row in a similar fashion while John opened the package of Jonafree scion wood and passed a twig to me.

"Take your pocketknife and make a long, diagonal cut. Make the surface of the wood flat. You want the angle to be smooth so it has the most contact possible with the tree. You need the two cambium layers to adhere."

The cambium layer is the two-celled thin membrane between the bark and the wood. It's the circulatory system of the tree. The cambium layer of the scion twig must match the cambium layer of the tree; the cells of both rapidly dividing as part of their natural spring growth will ensure they fuse completely.

Denis took a piece of scion wood, made an angle cut, shaving it clean with ease. Both John and Denis had no problem, but I was awkward with the knife, trying to hold the branch and cut the wood cleanly without shredding my hand.

Denis smiled at me. "It takes practice," he said with his piece of angled scion wood in his mouth.

"Now, shorten your piece." John added. "You only need one or two buds for the scion wood to grow."

John then showed me how to make vertical cuts around the circumference of the sawn trunk through the bark just deep enough to feel resistance from the wood of the tree. He peeled back the bark on each side of the cut and showed me how to slip my piece of scion wood into the opening. Denis slipped the piece from his mouth into the opening next to mine. When I asked him why he put it in his mouth, he shrugged, "I always do."

When we finished inserting six pieces of scion wood around the trunk, we wrapped white nylon tape tightly around the outside to secure the grafts. Lastly, we painted tree tar, a waxy material, on the bare wood of the trunks and on the tops of the twigs of scion wood to keep them from drying out. "In one year," John said, "a scion can become a five-foot-tall leafy branch. In two years it may be larger than many young trees, and by year three, if all grows well, it will start to bear fruit." This fast growth occurs because a large root system is already well established.

I checked on the grafts every few days. After only a few weeks the scion wood buds had put out leaves. The scions had mated with the trunk, nutrients were flowing into the buds, pushing out new growth. The grafts had taken. With Denis's help identifying all the trees, I made a new map of the orchard and included John's new varieties. My neighbor, Ed Baron, offered to put it all into a Microsoft Excel file, and we've been updating this map ever since.

While cross-pollinating was happening in the orchard, it was happening in other parts of my life. Muscular and suntanned, Blase wore his graying hair pulled back. I was so mesmerized by his deep voice that I often missed his actual words. Years before, Blase and his woodworking partner built a library for Paul in our home in Groton. I caught sight of him during the weeks they were installing the walnut cabinets, but I never said more than a brief hello. I met him once again, a year before I moved to the farm, at a summer picnic. Ariel was somewhere with Paul, and I found myself sitting with a plate of salad opposite Blase and his best friend, Ron. I don't remember what we talked about, but when they got up to go, I remember thinking: *These two men are going to change my life.* Darkness fell, and Paul, Ariel, and I stayed for a bonfire.

I had no other contact with Blase until after I had moved to the farm. We bumped into each other at a local food store, and I told him we had moved to Harvard. He asked incredulously, "You left the church?"

"Yes, I left the church. Paul and I have separated." I gave him my new address on a scrap of paper.

During the next week, Ariel and I decided to treat ourselves to a lobster dinner. I called Blase and invited him. I knew Ariel felt the excitement in my voice, and we were both disappointed when he turned me down because of a meeting he couldn't reschedule. During the next few weeks, our calendars left little room to get together. I told him I had an opening for an exhibit of sculpture in Concord, New Hampshire, the following Sunday and he said he would like to meet me there. After the opening, we went for pizza. Blase had driven there directly from a men's weekend he was teaching in western Massachusetts. I had no idea what he was talking about.

"It's a program for men that questions traditional ideas of being male and explores new ones," he explained. "We do all kinds of exercises to help men connect with buried feelings that affect their behavior and relationships. I got involved in the program when I was going through my second divorce, and it changed my life. Even though I had custody of my two children and it was hard to find childcare, one weekend a month I would attend the nine-month training program. Now I'm one of the facilitators."

After an hour of easy banter about one thing and another, Blase looked at me and asked, "What's going on here?"

I paused. I knew what he was asking. We were definitely doing the dance of getting to know each other.

Blase and Ron lived together across town. Both single, heterosexual men, they decided to share a house when Blase's children moved back with their mother. Almost everyone thought Blase and Ron were a couple, and they enjoyed keeping people guessing. Sometimes I stopped by in the morning after dropping Ariel at the school bus. They were usually sitting on the floor, Ron drinking tea and Blase drinking coffee, reading Rumi, Rilke, or Mary Oliver's poetry. They seemed to have plenty of time to chat. Shafts of morning sun flooded the modern glass room as Blase's yellow-nape Amazon parrot, Orco, chattered away, holding his own private telephone conversation (Hello! All right! Okay!). Nearby, a carved wooden Buddha from Indonesia sat with great equanimity.

A self-employed woodworker, Blase could make his own work hours. Ron, a retired chiropractor, was starting a new life after a divorce. Together they were teaching a course on emotional literacy at a local men's prison. The course helped the inmates understand their anger and what was behind it. With poetry, mythology, and group exercises Blase and Ron found ways for the men to access their emotions, be vulnerable, and share their grief.

Ron and Blase went to an African dance class on Thursday nights and their men's group met every other Monday night. I had entered a new world. When I was married, Paul and I went to classical music concerts and art openings. We were invited to gala celebrations at the National Gallery in Washington because Paul and the director at the time, J. Carter Brown, were childhood friends. I enjoyed attending these fancy dinners, mostly because we got to see some spectacular exhibits. The guest lists included donors to the museum and people who had lent art to the exhibitions. Inevitably the person sitting next to me would ask what I did, trying to figure out why I was there.

Hanging out with Blase and Ron, men my own age, felt right. They didn't care if I knew any important artists or even if I was an artist. They just seemed to like to chat with me and I with them. When they wanted to host a large community gathering at their house, I agreed to help. They had a wide circle of friends and invited dancers, carpenters, realtors, doctors, African drummers, and poets. Over a hundred people, most of whom I didn't know, gathered around a bonfire, recited poetry and prayers, and broke bread. The drums eventually came out, and either you were a drummer or a dancer. This willingness to give oneself to primal rhythms felt foreign to me. In mime and the Noh theater, the movements were always stylized and controlled. I wasn't used to letting my body find its own rhythm and express itself. Though I was among some great dancers that night, I found one's level of expertise didn't matter, and I opened myself to this new experience.

A few days later, when Blase and I were sitting on the front stoop at the farmhouse, I asked him, "When you die, if you were to come back as an animal, what would you like to be?"

I imagined he would say a lion or some other powerful creature.

"A swallow," he said after a moment's reflection.

"Why?"

He gazed up into the empty blue sky and smiled. "They're so playful."

When he asked me, I said, "A lion." I saw myself as needing to be strong. I didn't ever consider a playful life like a swallow's. Play was foreign to me. I had been a serious child and remained that way throughout my adolescence. Paul was serious; our life together was serious.

Part of the legacy from Paul's grandfather, Henri Matisse, was that you had to do something with your life and work hard at it every day. Paul told me about a visit to his grandfather when he was a young boy. Henri Matisse pointed him to a chair where he was to sit while his grandfather took up a stick of charcoal to draw his portrait.

My mother was also a role model of determination. Though I have photos from early in her first marriage, partying on New Year's Eve and fishing in Acapulco, for most of my life I remember she was always working hard to find her own path and make her own life. The sound of her electric typewriter as she wrote term papers and then her dissertation while I was falling asleep was a constant reminder of her single-minded resolve. As a woman developing her career later in life, she always said, "I had to work doubly hard."

Blase worked hard and played hard. He told me he and his five brothers woke at dawn when school was canceled for snow to get out early and shovel walks and driveways all day. In summer he climbed trees and biked all over Malden, a suburb of Boston. He always had jobs, carrying mortar, working in a burlap factory, and doing construction. He played football in high school and went to college on a football scholarship. He had stories of travels with his two bloodhounds, of old cars and trucks he'd owned, waiting tables, climbing mountains, girlfriends, and working in an oil field off the coast of Louisiana. He's a great lover of poetry and a spiritual seeker. When I told him that ever since I lived in Japan I wanted to return to walk one of the Buddhist pilgrimage trails, he said, "You should do it."

The most famous pilgrimage goes a thousand miles around the island of Shikoku. There are eighty-eight temples, and pilgrims stop at each one to say prayers. To do the whole circuit takes at least a month. While reading about the Shikoku pilgrimage, I found the book *Riding the Ox Home: Stages on the Path of Enlightenment*, a slender volume of ink drawings, poems, and commentary.

The Ox Herding series originated in China in the twelfth century, the creation of a Zen master to help his students understand the spiritual journey they were undertaking. Using the metaphor of an ox, a most valuable possession in ancient China, the journey begins when a young man, whip and tether in hand, heads off into the mountains to find his lost ox. He can't come home without it—the ox is his family's livelihood; it's used to plow the fields and its manure heats their home. After much searching, the young man notices a few hoof prints in the mud and knows he must be heading in the right direction. Next he catches sight of it from behind, a clear moment of recognition, but short-lived, for the ox quickly disappears. The young man doesn't give up and eventually catches the ox with his rope. Then the struggle really begins. It takes perseverance and training until the man and the ox finally walk together with ease.

I left my old life to end my suffering, but I didn't have an understanding of what I was seeking or where to find it. Do we really know what will make us happy? Or if we can find happiness and freedom in this lifetime? Like a bee flying from blossom to blossom, we hope each flower we encounter will bring satisfaction. But sometimes our longing seems insatiable. The unhappiness that led me to leave my marriage made me feel at times like the women characters in Noh plays who wear *hannya* masks, the ones with horns coming out of their head, women possessed by demons because of their jealousy or another "hungry ghost" obsession. Could I find that elusive freedom I remembered from my young and independent days? What had happened to make me feel trapped by my life instead of boldly living it? Reading *Riding the Ox Home: Stages on the Path of Enlightenment*, I identified with this story of a young man leaving home, setting out to search for something he was lacking, not returning home without it.

For much of my life, art had been my place of refuge and connection with my deepest longing, but I was realizing this was not enough. There was still something missing. Some question of who I really was and my place in the world. I was born Jewish and attended Hebrew School and synagogue with my family on important holidays. We were members of the oldest synagogue in Philadelphia, Rodeph Shalom, founded in

1795. The Moorish-style sanctuary as I remember it was an enormous sonorous space. When the adults stood around me to recite the Kaddish for those they were mourning, I remember a feeling of dropping into a dark cavern. The deep sounds of lamentation echoed inside my heart. Even today when I hear the Kaddish, I am still brought to tears.

The teachings we studied in Hebrew School had nothing to do with the ancient and mystical spirituality I connected with prayers like the Kaddish. When I was fourteen, I told my parents I didn't want to be confirmed. I didn't want to accept and enter the Jewish religion. They told me to talk with the rabbi. I made an appointment with the head rabbi, David Wice. We met in his tiny office, and I explained my reluctance. He didn't try to convince me to reconsider, but said with great kindness, "The door will always remain open." After that meeting, I was a person without a religion. But that didn't mean I wasn't still searching.

I discovered the author of the ox herding book was the Abbot of Zen Mountain Monastery in Mount Tremper, New York. The monastery website featured a one-week retreat titled "Wilderness, Art, and Zen," a camping canoe trip on Raquette Lake in the Adirondacks. Here was a retreat devoted to three things I loved, and it was scheduled for the week in August when the children would be on a vacation with Paul. It seemed more realistic than trying to return to Japan. Blase assured me he would look after the farm. I called Zen Mountain Monastery.

"I'm calling to sign up for the Wilderness retreat."

"Have you been to the monastery before?" a female voice asked.

"No, I just found the retreat listed on your website."

"Hmm, then you haven't attended our Introduction to Zen Training workshop?"

"No."

"Sorry," the efficient voice replied. "You have to first attend the weekend workshop before you can go on the Wilderness retreat. The next workshop is filled, but you can sign up for our July weekend."

"I can't do the July weekend," I said. I didn't tell her apple maggot fly traps go up in early July and the children . . . .

"Well," she continued, "we offer the Wilderness retreat every year."

"Isn't there some way I can go without doing the introductory retreat?" I asked.

"No, there isn't."

"Are you sure?" Uncharacteristically, I became a dog with a bone, and I wouldn't give it up.

Finally, the voice said, "There's nothing I can do, but you can talk with a teacher. Call back in ten days and ask for Shugen Sensei."

I hung up the phone and wrote Shugen Sensei a letter, including in the envelope some photos of my sculpture. I wanted to do everything I could to persuade him to let me go on the retreat.

Ten days later I called Shugen Sensei at the monastery.

"No," he said. "You cannot go on the Wilderness retreat without attending the Introduction to Zen Training."

"Isn't there some way?" I politely asked.

"No."

"Are you sure?"

"Yes."

I still did not want to give up. As someone who usually acquiesced to male authority and respected guidelines, I surprised myself by being so persistent. Trying to be strategic, I considered the matter from his perspective, wondering, *What is his concern?*

I tried a new tack. "I trained in the Noh theater in Japan for two years. I know a little about Zen."

"Zen isn't the issue," he said.

Ah, I realized, he is concerned *I may be afraid of spiders, or I may want to go home halfway through the trip.*

"I love the wilderness," I said next. "I've climbed all of the four thousand-footers in the White Mountains. I've summited Mt. Rainier, climbed in the Tetons, and backpacked through Peru."

"All right," he finally said reluctantly. "You can go on the Wilderness retreat." Then he added, referring to my sculpture, "By the way, I like your stuff."

Row 13: Orchard Pests

In early June, Denis showed me how to see how many blossoms were going to produce an apple by looking closely at the flower buds. The unpollinated buds went limp and fell from the tree with a little wind or a knock from my finger. But inside the pollinated buds, I could see the pillow-like stigmas had darkened and their supporting styles had grown more erect. These miniature clusters seemed to be reaching out to the sun, bursting with life. Then, within a few days, the base of the pollinated flowers would began to thicken, the ovary was growing, plumping into the unborn apple.

Meanwhile, the fiercest foe of New England apples, the plum curculio, was watching from the sidelines. Plum curculios are snout-nosed, hard-shelled beetles. They gather in the hedgerows around an orchard, mating and waiting for a warm night when the temperature is above seventy degrees and the fruit the size of green peas. Researchers at the University of Massachusetts believe the beetles travel back and forth from the woods to the orchard checking on the apples' progress, like scouts for an army. Then, at twilight, when all the elements align, the

Red-humped caterpillars

curculios fly into the orchard. The female, laden with eggs, lands on the apple, bites a small hole in the fruit, and deposits an egg. She then turns and makes a crescent-shaped cut around the cavity to keep the pressure of the growing apple from closing in and suffocating the developing larva. The egg incubates for a week, and then the newborn, footless larva burrows into the seed cavity where it eats and grows for another several weeks. The plum curculio will lay four or five eggs in an evening and up to two hundred eggs during her short life. There may be thousands of plum curculios on one tree. The males are out there, too, making small feeding pits on the fruit.

A nineteenth-century drawing shows a carpet spread under a tree and orchardists hitting the branches with hardwood paddles to make the plum curculios fall. The carpet prevents the larvae from entering the soil under the tree and pupating. Apparently, both movement and sound can make curculios fall out of a tree. I contemplated using some jarring music—would Stravinsky's *The Rite of Spring* do it? Or maybe we needed heavy metal, although my neighbor Ed might complain.

Denis had warned me that as much as ninety percent of a crop can be lost to this New England pest. Why was apple growing so difficult? The raspberries were doing well, the blueberries I planted were growing, and vegetables from the our kitchen garden kept us well fed, but these apples, the crop I had hung my hat on, remained elusive. And even more unnerving: I'd still been playing phone tag with the company that made our copper. I still hadn't received certification.

Commercial orchards spray pesticides to rid their orchards of the plum curculio beetle; organic orchardists have Surround. The discovery of Surround, which is refined kaolin clay, sprayed on the trees just after petal fall, is the only known organic solution for the plum curculio, and has made organic apple growing in New England possible. It also helps with other apple pests, such as codling moths and leafhoppers, but its primary use is to protect the young fruit from the stings of the plum curculio beetles.

Denis told me to keep a coating of Surround on the orchard from petal fall until the fruit was over an inch in size, from the end of April through mid-June, when the last of the plum curculios leave town. I used one hundred pounds to cover the two-acre orchard, applying three coats in quick succession to build up a good layer. Then I reapplied weekly, not only because rain washed the kaolin off the fruit but because the new growth of the apple had to be covered. Denis sent me an email in mid-June:

> I scouted the orchard last evening. I was pleased at the
> health and color of the foliage but disgusted at the
> PC presence and damage. As I walked around I saw
> numerous PCs actively feeding or laying eggs on fruit.
> Ed came out and I showed him the plum curculio . . . .
> For now I guess I would plan on selling your fruit for
> cider this season.

Ouch! I felt like I had been stung by a curculio. I was bitterly disappointed to receive Denis's email. He still wanted me to continue to apply Surround and to supplement it with another product, Entrust, an organic insecticide. These materials were expensive, and if I wasn't going to sell a crop it didn't make sense. But I wanted the orchard to succeed so I followed his suggestions. I had to face the fact it would take time to familiarize ourselves with the products available for organic growers and determine application rates and effectiveness. When I saw one of the little beetles sitting on an apple, I reminded myself I was not spraying Surround to kill the pest, just persuade it to choose some other host tree for its eggs—crabapples or wild plums.

With clay on the trees, the orchard had a ghostly appearance—leaves, branches, stems, and fruit glowed pale white. A cyclist, one who passed by almost every day on his spring training rides, stopped and asked me how it worked.

"First, it disguises the fruit and makes it hard to find," I told him. "And second, the grains of clay stick to the plum curculio's body, which they don't like. It's as if you came home from the beach still covered with sand."

"Do you wash it off the trees?"

"No, by harvest the residue is worn off from rain and wind."

"It's hard work," he noted. Before biking off, he told me he bought his apples from Whole Foods, but added, "I'll be back." ❀

Row 14: Perfect Fruit, Ugly Fruit

Over a century ago, the fruit growers of Montreuil, a town outside of Paris, well known for their early-season peaches grown along an intricate system of east-facing walls, grew prizewinning apples. I was interested in their techniques—they certainly didn't spray Surround.

During the winter months, women and children folded and glued paper bags making them from anything they could find—old receipts, train schedules, and pages ripped from a book. The apple crop grew enclosed in these bags, hidden from pests like Rapunzel in the witch's tower. The Montreuillois, wanting to further distinguish their fruit, developed a technique to stencil images using egg whites and snail slime. At the 1894 St. Petersburg Exposition, they showed off their stenciled apples, one prizewinner featured a portrait of the tsar of Russia.

Japanese orchardists developed their own technique of bagging apples. They sell these flawless fruits in elaborate gift boxes, the largest and most beautiful will be stenciled with sayings like, "Happy New Year, Sensei!" or "Congratulations, Yuki!" These gift apples can sell for $150 apiece. The perfect apple might then be cut into slivers and shared

Two-legged carrots for sale

with guests to toast the occasion.

The Japanese orchardists grow these apples by saving the king blossom and removing all the secondary flowers of each bud. As soon as the "king" is pollinated and the apple has begun to grow, the flower is enclosed in a specially designed, individual paper bag made with a double lining. The outer layer is opaque and the inner layer colored wax paper. The bag is folded to expand for the growth of the fruit, but sealed tightly with a wire to keep out the insects.

The fruit grows, checked by the orchardist several times during the maturation process. After three months, the outer bag is removed leaving only the wax paper. The pale and perfect fruit is now ready for the application of its stencil. Under the stencil, the apple skin is protected from light and will remain pale green, while the skin under the tinted wax paper begins to color rosy red.

The final step is to remove the wax paper and give the apple a little more time in the sun to finish its coloring and encourage the accumulation of sugars. The farmer rotates the apple to achieve a perfect uniformity of hue. Sometimes it's difficult to keep an apple turned in a particular direction. In this case the orchardist spreads reflective surfaces under the fruit and removes branches that might shade or cast shadows. Fruit bags are available on the internet, but they're expensive and would be impossible to use on a large crop. And I doubted our customers would appreciate a gift apple enough to pay $150.

In contrast to the Japanese cult of perfection, Isabel Soares started a cooperative in Lisbon called *Fruta Feia*, Ugly Fruit. Her work was a response to the restrictions the European Union dictates for the appearance of food—no curved cucumbers, no odd-shaped tomatoes. The amount of wasted food caused by these restrictions is staggering, so Soares and her colleagues were determined to buy produce that didn't make the grade from local farms and sell it much less expensively to members of their co-op. She estimated one-third of the food grown in Portugal was wasted because of both market and consumer standards. This alarming proportion holds true on the world scale, too. Despite how hard it is to grow food, one-third of the world's food production goes to waste annually.

One of Soares' farmers grows tomatoes in greenhouses where it's easier to control the growing conditions. Still, he said, about one-quarter of his tomatoes do not meet the standards of the supermarket chain he sells to. He is happy to sell his produce to the Ugly Fruit Cooperative at half the price. Soares wants to change "the dictatorship of perfection," that mindset which affects not only crop producers and regulators, but also customers who pass over dented apples at the supermarket.

Some young people in Germany opened stores specializing in "eccentric" fruit, selling it at a premium, filling their shelves with misshapen apples, tomatoes with little penises, and two-legged carrots, all actually quite common oddities you find when growing your own food.

In America companies are also trying to lessen food waste. Misfits Market sells "funny looking, always delicious" food. The company offers two sizes: their *Mischief* box feeds two people a week, and the *Madness* box feeds four or five. Prices are thirty to forty percent lower than in supermarkets. Sourcing their produce from farms in Pennsylvania and New Jersey, *Misfits Market* delivers by FedEx and UPS to most of the Eastern seaboard and plans to expand nationally.

Boston Area Gleaners in nearby Acton, Massachusetts, gleans annually over a million pounds of food from local fields and orchards and distributes this surplus to food banks, meal programs, and low-income markets. Their food is healthy and oftentimes simply surplus. A farmer doesn't always know when there will be a bumper crop of cauliflower or Brussels sprouts—too much for their local market.

It's not a new idea that our food choices will help save the planet. Fruitlands Museums, located in Harvard only a few miles from Old Frog Pond Farm, was the home of Bronson Alcott's experiment with intentional living. A radical thinker and one of America's most famous educators, Alcott wanted to bring positive change to the world with a new way of relating to the land. In 1843 Alcott brought his wife, Abigail, and their four daughters to live in a rundown farmhouse in Harvard

Vegan

where they were to follow a strict diet. They would eat only fruits and vegetables—live off the fruit of the land. They didn't wear clothing made of cotton because it was manufactured by slave labor and wool was out of the question, for that came from animals. Linen was the only option, cool in summer, but not helpful when the weather turned cold. The community didn't even use animals for plowing or manuring the fields which made the cultivation of enough land to feed even their small group impossible. Alcott believed following this strict regime would improve humanity by raising consciousness about how we were living in relationship to the earth and other beings.

This utopian experiment never grew beyond thirteen members, and when the weather got cold, they packed up and returned to Concord. Though the experiment failed, it did prefigure some of our contemporary vegetarian, vegan, and sustainable eating movements. Alcott's utopian community was doomed to failure because of his refusal to consider the realities of the deprivations he was demanding of his family. Today there are many more options for people who want to eat less meat and help reduce carbon emissions produced by massive cattle feed lots or resist eating genetically modified corn and grains.

The original Farmhouse at Fruitlands was part of the estate purchased in 1910 by Clara Endicott Sears (1863-1960), a prominent Bostonian who devoted her life to cultural preservation, literature, spirituality, and the arts. Sears lived in Groton in a large Revival-style house before moving to Harvard and building a new home on Prospect Hill. Sears named this new property "Fruitlands" because the farmhouse Alcott had used for his community was on the edge of her new land. Sears's interest in utopian communities led her to learn more about a radical religious sect, the Shakers, who had had a thriving community in Harvard in the mid 1850s. By the early 1900s, with only a few elder members still practicing (the Shakers were celibate), they needed to sell off some of their buildings. Sears purchased the oldest one and moved it to Fruitlands to become part of her new museum. Finding Native American artifacts on her property led her to acquire a significant collection of related artifacts, and she built a museum to exhibit them. Her interest in art continued to broaden to include primitive portraits as well as Hudson School paintings. Art, spirit, and landscape coexisted and complemented each other at Fruitlands. Shaker spirituality, Native American beliefs, and the Transcendentalist ideals are joined by a reverence for the land.

I met Maud Ayson, Fruitlands' executive director, a few of years after I moved to Old Frog Pond Farm. Maud came for a visit and sat with me on a large bench by the pond which I had made from a slab of rough-cut maple. She told me how difficult it was to attract visitors to the museums. People visited, saw the collections, and they didn't return unless they were bringing out-of-town guests. I proposed an exhibit that would relate to the land and also appeal to families. Using old agricultural tools I would create an outdoor installation of circus acts and call it "A Circus Comes to Fruitlands." She loved the idea, and I set to work.

The garage space I made into my shop was above the barn area where the Spauldings, the prior owners, had kept sheep. Here, under my studio, they had left all kinds of agricultural tools. I found an old cultivator and stood it on end, placing stones on the tines to make *The Juggler*.

A wagon wheel wrapped in bittersweet vines became the hoop for *Leon the Lion* to jump through. A bifurcated trunk from a tree beavers had taken down became the long legs for the *Reclining Stilt Man*. To make a big clown, I took the corn crib the Spauldings' sheep must have fed from, painted the slats, and standing it on end filled it with hay for the clown's body. When Caleb saw it, he suggested an old milk jug for the head and he brought it over the following day. I grabbed a sickle knife for a happy smile, bolts for eyes, and *Sweet Hay the Clown* arrived on stage. With an upside down cast iron teapot for a head and a large wooden ox yoke painted blue for its broad shoulders, a *Dancing Bear* stood on two legs. The wooden *Magician's Box* was pierced by two dozen hand saws, creating the illusion that the disappearing woman was somehow magically still alive inside.

These pieces were outdoor sculptures, built to weather New England elements. Inside the Alcott farmhouse I placed the delicate "acts." There was a baby elephant with a long articulated trunk, a trapeze artist swinging through the air, and a strong man squatting before a big lift in tight little bark shorts. Twenty-three circus acts in all. The museum staff designed a play area with push-the-hoop, pairs of stilts, and juggling balls for children to play. It was the museum's first contemporary art exhibit. Maud held the exhibit over for a second year, and a new tradition of contemporary sculpture at Fruitlands was established. Boston sculptor Joseph Wheelwright's monumental *Tree Figures* followed the "circus" as the outdoor exhibit for the next two years, bringing large crowds from Boston to see his amazing art.

While working on the "circus" I focused on what kind of humor and wit I could offer the museum visitors. The circus theme connected me back to my mime days in college, and training in Paris at the *École Internationale de Théâtre Jacques Lecoq*. Working on this exhibit had many parallels with life on the farm. Farmers save everything. I would always look for what I needed. Nuts and bolts came out of one object to be used in another. I learned to weld and cut metal so I could take apart old tools and put them back together in new ways. When the "circus" sculptures came back to the farm I put some of them out in the orchard and on the trails. The following season I invited sculptor friends to bring their own work. Old Frog Pond Farm's annual outdoor sculpture exhibit has been going on ever since.

Meanwhile, I was still waiting to hear about the copper. And Don Franczyk, head of Baystate Organic Certifiers, was waiting to hear from me. I needed that certification. Don has been in this business since the 1980s—first as a farmer and then heading the certification process for the New England Farming Association's (NOFA) Massachusetts chapter in the 1990s. When I spoke with him he said his hands were tied.

It seemed like a small technicality. Our apples were growing! Green fruitlets hung from the trees in clusters. The damage Denis had identified turned out to be less than he surmised. The June drop, a natural phenomenon when the tree lightens its load, had taken care of a good number of the diseased apples. But we hadn't yet reached anyone sympathetic at the company that made our copper. I now knew firsthand why some growers disparage the organic system. We were wedged between regulations, and there was no way to convince Don Franczyk that our product should be approved. If our apples weren't certified as organic, there would be limited opportunity to market them. Old Frog Pond Farm was a small hole-in-the wall operation compared to Harvard's three large orchards. We had no agri-tainment—no moonwalk, hayrides, or corn maze, not even cider donuts.

I was convinced from my exposure to the collective wisdom at the Holistic Apple Growers meeting that growing food without synthetic pesticides and herbicides needed to become the norm worldwide. It was the only way to protect our soils and water supplies.

And I was ready to convince anyone who asked. I had seen firsthand why people who say you can wash the fruit are mistaken. When spraying the orchard I watched how the sprays covered every leaf, fruit, and branch to the point of runoff. The droplets fell to the ground and were absorbed into the soil. Plants took up whatever was in the soil. Whatever we sprayed was inside the fruit.

Organic food sells at a premium and not everyone can afford to buy it, but I was realizing organic didn't need to be more expensive. Whether a conventional or organic orchardist, we both had to buy expensive spray material for our orchards. I resolved to price my apples according to what I needed to keep the orchard going rather than charge a high price simply because the fruit was organic.

Some farmers complain that certification is too expensive. However, in Massachusetts, the Commonwealth reimburses fifty percent of the cost. For example, the 2021 certification cost for a new farm with an income between $30,000 and $40,000 is $800. With the reimbursement from the state, the cost is $400. Still, some people are adamant they don't want to follow any more regulations than they already have to. I could sympathize, but our farm depended on receiving organic certification.

Our crop was sizing up.

It was a great relief when a friend who was helping me discovered our copper product, while not on the current OMRI list, was on an older one. I called our certifier, right away. "That's good," Don said, "but the product might have changed—otherwise, why isn't it on the current list? If the material is the same as on the older list, you need to get the company to state that fact in writing."

My calls to the company continued to get me nowhere. I would leave my name and wait for a call back and I wouldn't hear anything. Then I'd call back and start over with a new person. I was riding an organic certification roller coaster. *Couldn't Don understand that we were growing healthy apples?* ❧

Row 15: Wilderness and Zen Training

In July, throughout the orchard I hung Apple Maggot Fly traps, red plastic balls on bright yellow cards covered in Tangle Trap, a sticky, gooey material. I didn't know what this insect did to the fruit, but its name sounded quite awful. The red and yellow colors along with scented bait lure insects to the fake apple. They stick to it and die. Commercial orchards put out one or two traps an acre to determine the insect pressure and decide when and what to spray, but we hang them all around the periphery to lure as many apple maggot flies as possible to the trap. There is no organic material labeled for use against this pest.

I learned to identify the apple maggot fly by the black-and-white zigzag pattern on their wings, but the traps attracted everything, flies, ants, moths. It wasn't an exact science and not at all comforting to see wings, legs, bodies, and assorted other insect parts stuck in the Tangle Trap goo. I never found more than a few apple maggot flies. At the end of the season, I took down the traps and scrubbed the yellow cards and red balls with mineral oil to remove the sticky coating. It was messy and time consuming. I wondered if I needed to take this pest seriously.

Riding the Ox Home, sculpture, 2010   Photo: Joe Ofria

A few years later, I received an email from Michel Phillips, the organizer of the Holistic Apple Meeting, saying, "Seriously, I got through ninety-five percent of the growing season with a very clean crop, but AMF [apple maggot fly] has devastated everything. I was on top of trap timing and quite sure more than two thousand flies have been put to rest. But they keep on coming . . . ."

Our orchards are unique ecosystems, in the same way our bodies are unique bodies. What's good for one may not be beneficial for another. The set of issues we confront are different. It must have been a bumper year for apple maggot flies in northern New Hampshire, but I learned from experience we didn't have apple maggot fly pressure in our orchard. At least not yet.

In early August, when our apples were developing their sugars and my children were on vacation with Paul, it was time for the wilderness retreat, the one Shugen Sensei had let me sign up for. I was reluctant to leave the farm, but Blase, as promised, would keep an eye on everything. I was shocked at the detailed list of what each of us must bring. It was very, very specific: one pair of pants, one pair of shorts, closed-toe shoes, a knife with open blade and sheath that could be strapped onto a belt, and all the food I would need for the week. We would be preparing our meals separately at our own campsites.

I drove to the monastery, and from there our group of twelve attendees carpooled to the Adirondacks. I shared the trip with another participant, Francis Patnaude, a sculptor, and a perfect traveling companion. He had been a student at the monastery for almost ten years and I pummeled him with questions. The rest of the trip we talked about art.

Upon arrival in upstate New York, we loaded our gear into canoes and paddled an hour north to our main campsite. From there we were each directed towards a tent site where we were to set up our own camp. Mine was close to a pine tree near a blanket of moss with flat stones leading to the lake. It reminded me of Japan. I hadn't felt the solitude of being alone in nature since living in that single tatami mat room in a small temple in Kyoto. Boiling water on a camp stove and sipping tea,

I returned to conversations begun with my old Zen companion poets. The retreat was designed to be a combination of solitary time and group activities.

Shugen Sensei and Hojin, a senior monastic, were the leaders. Shugen had a joyful, clear face. He had the air of an expert Boy Scout leader. Hojin was slight, like an elf. She had been a professional potter before becoming a monk. She gave each of us a stack of watercolor paper and a set of watercolors to use for the week. The next morning, after group meditation and a solitary breakfast, we paddled off in our canoes to paint. Hojin said, "Paint what you see, exactly what is in front of you—the reeds, the movement of water, the clouds." We dipped our brushes into the lake, I dipped my paper.

When we returned to our main campsite we spread our paintings on the ground to share. No comment, critique, or praise. It was just the doing and sharing of the work in silence. This approach intrigued me. Usually I would be judging my work, wanting it to be a certain way or to communicate something specific. Here, we would put our paintings out for everyone to see, and we would just walk around in silence, noticing, but not saying anything. We were not to distinguish, at least out loud, between a person who clearly had talent and experience from someone who didn't. In the silence we could watch our minds wanting to judge, choose and prefer, hold onto opinions.

On one memorable evening we got into our canoes with our art supplies. We painted as the setting sun hid the distant hills, then the nearer trees, and finally, even the shoreline. There, in the inky stillness, we dipped our brushes and stroked our paper. Painting in the darkness was freeing. The sound of lapping water hitting our canoes amplified the obscurity as we paddled back to camp.

On a rainy day we stayed in our tents, and were told to prepare a story to share with the group. It would be informal, but I remember writing and rewriting. I wanted my story to be good, to be as good as I could make it. Finally finished, I couldn't imagine telling it because every word mattered. I read it. When Shugen Sensei's turn came he started telling his story. Then, all of sudden, he stopped speaking. After a moment, and in answer to our quizzical faces, he concluded, "That's as far as I got."

I became aware of my desire to do things well. I began to ask myself whom I was trying to please. I started to see that this tendency prevented me from truly responding to what was in front of me. I had one foot on the process and another on the finished work. What would it be like to respond, to live, without self-censoring? Old habits are hard to break. On the last morning, I approached Shugen Sensei's tent site while he was stirring oatmeal over his cookstove and said, "I'm ready to pursue Zen practice. I've started a new life, and I am trying to take responsibility for it."

"Good," he said. "Sign up for the Introduction to Zen Training weekend."

I signed up for the weekend retreat. Thirty of us checked in, filling out a short form marking any special needs we had and what we did for work. I wrote down "artist and orchardist." That evening, we sat together in the spacious meditation hall. The next morning, after a period of meditation and breakfast, a bell rang for an hour and a half of work practice.

Work practice happens every day for every member of the community. It's as serious as meditation practice and takes place in silence. We were each assigned a task, and our instructions were to focus completely on the job—whether cutting carrots in the kitchen, bringing in firewood, or cleaning bathrooms. The silence would give us the opportunity to watch our minds; to see all the commenting and rambling thoughts we fabricate unceasingly, especially when we are silent.

The work practice supervisor assigned me to look at some apple trees. Five sad young trees stood in a cluster not far from the main building, a gift from a student to the monastery. They hadn't grown much in the three years since they had been planted. Deer had repeatedly eaten their branches, and the only solution was to place fencing around each tree. But a more serious problem was the soil. The trunks moved with the lightest touch. The trees were standing in wet clay; their roots had no anchor. *Good thing we don't have soil like this at the farm.* I wondered how anything could grow in it. I suggested they all be transplanted to somewhere less wet, and on my next monastery visit I was given a crew and the work assignment to replant them.

After work practice we gathered in the meditation hall to listen to Daido Roshi, the Abbot of the monastery. He was a formidable presence, in colorful robes, sitting on a raised dais. We listened to him tell the story of Siddhartha, the man who became the Buddha. It's a story I have read and heard innumerable times, but each time I am inspired anew.

In his classic book, *Old Path White Clouds: Walking in the Footsteps of the Buddha,* Thich Nhat Hanh tells how Siddhartha was born into a royal family. After his birth, a holy man proclaimed the baby would become a great ruler or a great religious teacher. His father, the king, was determined to do everything possible to influence his son to follow in his own footsteps.

He showered upon Siddhartha every extravagance to induce his only son and heir to choose a royal life. He tried his best to shield Siddhartha from the suffering of life outside the palace walls. But the young Siddhartha loved to go outside the palace, visit villages, and talk with wandering monks. On these outings he saw the realities of old age, sickness, and death. Questions formed in his mind. Why was there so much suffering? What is the meaning of life if it ends with old age and death?

Siddhartha married, delighting his father who thought his son would now surely remain in the palace and, someday, become king. However, the young couple continued to visit the villages, doing what they could to ease the pain and suffering they encountered. Though Siddhartha must have enjoyed the sweetness of his newly married life, seeing so much sickness and death overwhelmed him. He had to find answers to his questions. On the night Siddhartha's own son was born, his joy was mixed—happiness at the birth of his son and grief for the suffering he knew would follow. A few weeks later, in the middle of the night, he asked his faithful servant to saddle his horse and ride with him far into the countryside. Siddhartha sent his companion back to the palace with both horses and his royal robes. He remained alone in the forest with only a white cotton cloth to cover his body. He left family, wealth, and status to become a seeker, a beggar clothed in rags, an ascetic determined to find the truth of what it means to be human.

Daido Roshi talked about the pain and suffering we all feel, the undercurrent of discontent that afflicts many of us, even if we think we are happy. He spoke of feelings of separation and emptiness and our desire to live meaningful lives. He expressed his pain for the destruction of the earth, and for all those suffering on the planet. "Let the mountains and rivers be your teachers," he said. I started weeping, deeply touched by his words. *Why am I here? What is the meaning of my life? What am I looking for? What am I missing?* I raised my hand with a question I was trying to form. *What did the Buddha discover? Can I discover it?* But I was crying so hard and only said, "How? I can't live here. I live far away."

He said, "There are many lay practitioners who come to the monastery when their work and family life allows. You can do this."

Daido Roshi had seen responses similar to mine many times during his years as abbot. When someone is touched by the teachings of Buddhism, it's like a bolt of lightning in the night sky. The magnitude of the void is frightening. I didn't know anything. My pain was ruthlessly exposed.

I hadn't signed up to have my world gutted open. Now what was I going to do?

Later, in the dining room, Daido Roshi came over to me.

"Are you okay?"

I nodded.

"What do you do?"

"I'm an artist and a farmer."

"What kind of art?"

"I use agricultural tools and found objects."

He was gentle, but offered no answers.

After lunch and a short rest period, we gathered for a taste of art practice. Hojin, the senior monastic who had led the painting practice on the wilderness retreat, provided us with paper, ink brushes, and small yogurt containers with black ink. She told us first we were going to paint the most beautiful picture we could imagine.

"Take a few breaths and imagine your scene—mountains or rivers, the ocean, your children—and then begin to paint. But," she added with a smile, "don't put any ink on your brush."

Surprised, we painted our masterpieces, flourishing our brushes here and there. Next she directed us in a series of exercises.

"Fill the page with horizontal lines. Take another page and do the same. Use all the paper you want."

She loosened our arms, and our fears at the same time.

"Make circles now," she said.

"Now, make one large circle on the page. Do it again, and again. Pay attention to your breathing, to your bodies. Relax."

"Now," she said, as the room grew quiet, "Paint the beautiful picture you first imagined." I painted an apple tree.

After art practice ended, we had a little time to walk the grounds. A light supper was followed by evening meditation. On Sunday morning Daido Roshi gave a formal talk. Then we shared a community spaghetti lunch, a tradition from his Italian upbringing.

In my reading about apple pollination, I had learned even the apple varieties that don't require cross-pollination have a better fruit set when they are cross-pollinated. I had experienced the power of a group sharing a common intention. This was *Sangha*, one of Buddhism's three treasures, the group of people who practice together, a treasure because we need each other. Like stones in a rock tumbler, living in a close community, relationships are not always easy: it takes polishing to shine, and we need others to make this happen.

As I drove home, I felt cut off from this comradery of fellow seekers. After the intensity of the weekend, I felt like I had left part of myself at the monastery. We were all on this journey together, but leaving reminded me that we each make the journey alone. It made me think of the farm in a new way. *Could Old Frog Pond Farm become its own nourishing community?*

Row 16: Miracle Apples

The artist <u>Yoko Ono</u> translated from Japanese to English a book about an orchardist, Akinori Kimura, and put it on her "Imagine Peace" website. She believed Kimura's story of growing apples without chemical pesticides should be shared with the world outside of Japan. She wrote, "If his method is used to raise fruits and vegetables, it will save our children, our grandchildren, and us from getting unnecessary illness. That's why I call this book a revolution."

Living in Aomori Prefecture where forty percent of Japan's apples are grown, Kimura cultivated his apple trees with chemical pesticides and fertilizers like his neighboring orchardists. He sprayed by hand, not having fancy equipment, and when pesticides splashed onto his skin, the irritation was so bad some of his flesh would strip off. His wife developed terrible skin rashes to the sprays. In light of these dangerous reactions, Kimura resolved to phase out all insecticide sprays.

The first few years, he only cut back on the chemicals, and his trees adapted to the lower rate, but when he quit spraying altogether, the trees developed a bacterial disease causing them to drop all of their leaves.

Our miracle apples

That was the end of fruit production. Kimura, not wanting to return to chemicals, tried to find an alternative. He sprayed garlic, salt, and distilled alcohol, but nothing worked. He sprayed diluted vinegar and continued to mow the weeds around his trees, but the trees still didn't bear fruit. The other apple growers, who in the beginning thought he was crazy, now became angry, fearing the bacteria in his orchard would contaminate their trees. Neighbors called him a failure. As Kimura sank deeper and deeper into debt, dragging his wife, elderly parents, and children along with him, he became desperate. He realized they would be better off without him and resolved to take his life.

One evening, the moon shining, with rope in hand, he headed into the mountains. As he tried to toss the rope over a large branch, it fell to the ground. When he went to retrieve it, he saw an apple tree glowing in the moonlight. Kimura wondered why an apple tree was growing so high up on the mountainside. He was amazed. It seemed healthy and free of pest damage. Kimura headed home that evening full of hope.

When he returned the next day to see the apple tree, he realized he'd been mistaken. It was a small oak. As he explored around its trunk, reaching through tall weeds, he found that the soil was rich and crumbly. This was his *aha* moment. The answer was in the soil. The imagined apple tree had saved him. With this insight, Kimura realized he had always looked above ground for solutions. He reasoned if he could replicate this fertile environment of rich soil and weeds, his apple trees would also be healthy.

Kimura enriched the soil by planting soybeans under his trees and letting the weeds and grasses grow naturally. He sprayed a vinegar solution in early spring, an antiseptic for the orchard to knock down disease. It took two more seasons of experimentation. Finally, seven years after he had stopped using pesticides, Kimura had his first crop. The fruit was small, but it was a harvest nonetheless. The populations of microorganisms living under his trees had made the transition to natural farming possible. Scientists later studied his soils and found the organisms to be similar to those found in old-growth forests.

Over the next twenty years, Kimura's trees continued to be healthy and bear delicious fruit. People called them "miracle apples." It had taken time for his orchard's transition. The soil microbiology, the bacterial and fungal populations, the nematodes, the mycelium, all needed to establish themselves before they could provide the minerals and nutrients needed by his trees. The trees, in turn, had to learn to use the microbiology in the soil, rather than rely on chemical feedings.

Not all growers would have had Kimura's determination and faith, especially while he caused so much suffering to his family. Kimura's story inspired me. I wanted to grow fruit in the most natural way possible. But I also needed our organic certification.

September arrived and the farm had a crop of apples. Fruit hung from branches on trees in almost every row. The Golden Delicious and the Blushing Golden had by far the most apples and the fruit was clean. I called Carlson's Orchards and told Frank I had apples for him. He said come over and pick up an empty crate. One of his men loaded a forty-bushel wooden bin into the bed of Blase's pickup truck, filling it entirely. A bushel is forty pounds: the crate would hold eight hundred pounds of apples. I drove through the orchard, handpicked enough fruit to fill the bin, and delivered the apples to Carlson's the next day.

Frank seemed a little nervous about my arrival.

"It's our inspection day," he said. "The organic inspector will be here shortly."

When I told him our organic certification was still in process, his face dropped. He told a forklift operator to unload my pickup and slip the crate off to the side. I got the message: I needed to disappear. I'm glad he didn't send me home with almost a thousand pounds of fruit I would have had to unload apple by apple. When I called later, Frank told me he didn't use our apples in his organic cider and could only pay me two dollars a bushel—the wholesale price for conventional cider apples, the lowest grade. Needless to say, I was disappointed. That would never work. With such a small orchard I would need to grow a healthy crop and sell all our apples for eating.

I called the company who made the copper product again. Finally I reached a man who explained the product was changed to a different label due to a "consolidation of product line." The EPA number remained the same on both labels, and neither the active nor inert ingredients had changed. Whew! He also said the company didn't put the product on the OMRI list because the paperwork was so arduous. He would send a note to our certifier. I had reached a real person, a sympathetic person.

Old Frog Pond Farm officially received its organic certification a few weeks later. The first crop was celebratory, but financially a bust. I sold some fruit to the folks who came to pick raspberries, and picked all I could to bake, sauce, dry, and freeze, but much of the fruit stayed on the trees. Because of the timing I hadn't been able to create a market. Old Frog Pond Farm had grown a crop of organic apples, but we were not on the map for the general public. What I didn't yet know was the first year's fruit would be the cleanest and easiest to grow. While the public didn't yet know about our orchard, neither did the insects. ❧

Row 17: Grafting a Relationship

Blase and I continued to see each other. We talked about his mother's Russian farm family who had immigrated to America, leaving before Stalin's purges, and settled on land in Glendale, Arizona. His father's family was from Naples, and Blase loved to talk about his Italian grandfather, Biaggio, who lived across the street from his parents' home in Malden, Massachusetts. Biaggio grew pears, peaches, cherries, and grapes in his small front yard. When Blase was young, his grandfather would say, "Pick up the drops, those are the ripe ones. Don't pick fruit from the tree."

On Saturday mornings, Blase's father piled the older boys along with Biaggio into an old Rambler station wagon and drove to Haymarket Square in Boston. "Biaggio carried brown paper bags, ones he could make last two years," Blase told me. "He filled them up with mushrooms, provolone cheese, chestnuts, and peppers. Rainy days were the best because the vendors sold everything cheap to get rid of it quickly. My grandmother would make fresh ravioli, stuffed mushrooms, and sauce for Sunday lunch."

Blase's potato heart, 2009

Blase still lived with Ron on the other side of town, but he was spending more and more time at the farm. He thought I should plant more varieties of fruit trees. What about plums? And hazelnuts? And more peaches? I had already planted three peaches and three pears. My first reaction was, No, no. I'm in over my head already. But I went ahead and ordered two hazelnut trees, two plums, two more peaches, and twelve Asian pears, along with some new apple varieties.

I loved hanging out with Blase. He had a rustic place on the marsh in Rowley, north of Boston, a cabin without electricity or running water. We would drive up, kayak through the estuaries, or take his little metal skiff out with Lucille, his big bloodhound sitting shotgun. When the tide was out we would strip naked and take mud baths. My life became rooted more and more in the natural world, while Blase started to put down his own roots at the farm. He enlarged the kitchen garden. When he dug up our first potato he brought me a heart-shaped potato and another with a small penis. They stayed on the kitchen windowsill behind the sink all winter. In the spring, we finally cooked and ate them.

Blase created a sacred space in the large field across the pond for bonfires and ceremonies. He mapped out a fifty-five-foot circle, and along its perimeter dug in eight large plinths of granite, each one rising six to eight feet above ground, marking the cardinal directions, north, south, east, and west, and the directions in between each one. In the center he placed a circle of stones for a fire pit. On the winter solstice over a hundred friends joined us as we lit a warming bonfire, the sparks shooting high into the night sky. People brought poems to share, songs, and a masked wolf recited one of Rilke's *Duino Elegies*. Afterwards we all gathered in the farmhouse for a potluck feast and music-making. The kitchen I so loved when I first visited the farm expanded to welcome the crowd. On every surface were pots and plates of food, and the open shelves made it easy for everyone to find a bowl, plate, or cup. Our first solstice celebration made me realize the farm was nurturing a community of people who felt its offer of connection and sustenance, both physical and spiritual.

Blase, supportive of my Zen practice and a meditator himself, transformed a small shack on the edge of the orchard into a meditation hut. I named it the Heron Hut after the squawking herons that fly by and fish in the wetlands. In the morning I walk through the orchard to the hut to meditate. Some days fellow sitters from neighboring towns join me, other times I sit alone. There's no electricity hum—only the caws and chirps of the birds, rain on the roof, wind, and the occasional bark of a neighbor's dog. Once when I was sitting alone I felt the presence of some other being. I stood up and slowly made my way to the window. There a silver coyote stood motionless in a foot of snow. We looked at each other for a few minutes, then it loped off. I think it must have been sleeping under the hut and woke up, sensing my presence.

In February in thick snow, Denis and I pruned. I continued to marvel at his fluidity in making pruning cuts. We enjoyed our time together. I returned in March to the holistic apple meeting by myself. I was now treated as an organic apple grower, and I was happy to be in the company of this apple community. Michael Phillips had worked out a protocol for four "health supporting" spring sprays, all using neem oil. Neem is an evergreen tree that is native to southern India. Its medicinal uses can be found in medical texts as early as 4000 B.C.E. The Neem tree's Sanskrit name means, "to give good health." Michael certainly believed this to be so. He also suggested we avoid sulfur sprays completely or at least limit them. Instead of focusing on the need to get rid of the "bad" fungi, we would better serve our trees by cultivating and supporting the beneficial ones. If enough "good" fungi colonized our leaves, scab wouldn't be a problem. Like a nutritionist's suggestion to eat fermented food in order to have a rich diversity of biology in our gut, Michael's suggestions were always about promoting health in the orchard, not fighting disease. His suggestions aligned exactly with what I had learned from the story of Kimura's "miracle" apples.

I took Michael's suggestion to use neem oil and ordered enough for several sprays. Using a clean five-gallon bucket I mixed warmed neem, warm water, and Dr. Bonner's soap to disperse the oil in the water. Then, it all went into the spray tank. Before I finished the first row, the spray nozzles had clogged. I climbed down from the tractor seat and cleared the nozzles with my paperclip. I cleared them over and over as I drove through the rows. When the spraying was finished, I opened the lid to the spray tank and peered inside. Neem oil about a half-inch thick coated the inside walls of the tank. I had no choice but to climb inside and scrape away the waxy layer with a metal spatula from the kitchen. Neem oil was caked in my hair, and its pungent scent penetrated so deeply into my nose, I thought I would never stop tasting it.

I wrote to Michael about my experience. He replied, "You have to be careful when mixing the neem to make sure it's in full suspension before it goes into the tank." He suggested I use a stronger soap. Michael doesn't certify his orchard, so while he grows the healthiest fruit he can, he's not worried about minute amounts of a synthetic material that may be in the eco-soap he uses. When I asked my certifier about several stronger yet environmentally friendly soaps, he couldn't approve them because each one contained trace amounts of a synthetic material used in the processing. There are times when being certified is absolutely frustratingly ridiculous, and this was one of them. At the time, Dr. Bonner's was the only soap on the OMRI list. Michael believed Neem oil was worth the trouble, but I gave up on it.

Since I couldn't figure out the neem, I couldn't follow Michael's four holistic sprays, but I decided I would limit my sulfur use, and add liquid fish and seaweed for nutrition, as well as compost teas. I followed the charts in Michael's book, *The Holistic Apple Grower*, and calculated the scab spore release based on temperatures and wetting period. I applied sulfur only when there would be a large spore release. It was a calculated risk, but one I felt worth taking. I wanted to grow healthy trees and offer healthy fruit to the public.

Occasionally I would stop over at Frank Carlson's. He would say, "I should have sprayed earlier, but the rain came and we couldn't get out and spray or "Oh, we lost a block of such and such." I was beginning to see that no matter whether you grow organic apples or follow conventional protocols, there is no promise of success. Drought one season, too much rain in another, freezing temperatures, hail, even changes in regulations, all challenge the grower. ❋

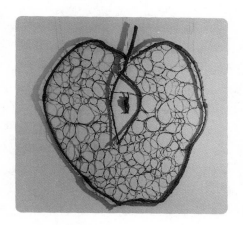

Row 18: Art in the Orchard

Eager to encourage more artists to come to the farm, I asked a friend, Alicia Dwyer, if she would teach a drawing workshop in the orchard. She agreed, and we set a date for early May. Alicia chose a Vincent Van Gogh drawing of an apple tree in bloom to advertise the class. She wanted to teach when the blossoms were open.

Blossoms were late that year. That was no problem for Alicia, instead she had us focus on the bark. Eight of us found ourselves on a chilly afternoon sitting on milk crates with drawing boards, paper, clips, and an assortment of pens, pencils, and charcoal, gazing intently into the trees. To most people's surprise the bark was mottled gray, not at all brown like one would expect. And the trees were crazy looking—leaning in one direction, and then going off diagonally in another. In order to compose a drawing where the tree didn't look like it was falling down, your eye had to bring the tree back to a state of equipoise. I thought of Noh dancers striking energetic poses. Some trees were warriors, while others were graceful maidens about to take flight.

Being out in the orchard as an artist, not on the seat of the tractor or

From One Seed, *sculpture with Gabrielle White, 2017*

with a pruning saw, I could just sit and follow Alicia's directions. Each tree had a story to tell. I wasn't there to worry about their health, only to see their shapes and express their unique vigor, along with the other artists.

After our drawing exercises, Alicia gave us thin pieces of tin and metal tools to "draw" into them, pressing our lines as if embossing an etching. Then we took paint and rubbed it into the tin surface, filling in the lines with ink and wiping off the surface. The tin was a great medium to capture the bark of the old trunks. Its surface looked like water flowing down a mountain stream.

Ten days after Alicia's workshop, the weather warmed, the buds opened. The orchard, however, wasn't the extravagant show of the year before. The Golden Delicious trees, in particular, had fewer blossoms. I was seeing firsthand the importance of thinning the fruit.

Thinning is how an orchardist controls a tree's propensity for biennial production. Most people confuse thinning with pruning. Thinning is the removal of either blossoms or young fruit to control apple production. Thinning regulates how many apples the tree will bring to maturity, which in turn determines the size of the fruit. The more apples on the tree, the smaller each one will be. Too much fruit, and branches might break. When the apples are close together, pests and disease show up exactly where they touch.

Apple trees decide their fruit set in July for the following year. When the trees are carrying a large bumper crop of apples, many varieties decide to have a light crop for the next season. It's a form of survival of the species; the tree isn't concerned with growing apples, but in producing seeds. If there's plenty, they take a needed rest. Thinning the fruit in June lets a tree know not to let up, to continue to produce seed because the orchardist has removed some of its future potential.

Commercial orchards begin their thinning when blossom petals begin to fall, and they use chemical materials not approved for an organic orchard. They spray to destroy a percentage of the blossoms and then a few weeks later, they reapply if necessary. Timing is crucial. Cold temperatures inhibit the efficacy of these sprays and too much heat can make them too effective. An orchardist doesn't want to leave too much fruit, nor get rid of too much. It's nerve-racking. Denis hadn't emphasized the importance of thinning our first year. But now he gave me instructions to begin in June when the apples would be about a half-inch in diameter.

I started with the small trees, experimenting both with a scissors and using my thumbnail to cut through the apple stem. When I approached the larger trees, my focus was on getting rid of diseased fruit. They were easy to spot because a yellow-orange goo would be oozing from a small hole and staining the immediate area around the opening. A larva was inside eating away. When I inadvertently left a five-gallon bucket with diseased fruit on our porch overnight, the next morning I saw the mass of small larvae moving. They had hatched and were crawling around in the white bucket. Had I left these apples on the trees, these larvae would be crawling around in the soil under the trees preparing to pupate.

However, the task of hand-thinning the big old, mature trees seemed ridiculous. I could have spent every daylight hour picking off fruit and not come close to making a difference. I gave up thinning the mature trees. I would have needed a crew of helpers, and I had a project in the studio to complete.

Influenced by Blase's devotion to *A Course in Miracles,* a book that teaches a spiritual journey using Christian language, I found myself reading about the "Via Cruces," Stations of the Cross, the Christian spiritual journey. I was carrying a lot of guilt after the breakup of my marriage. The past didn't go away just because I had moved to a new town. Believers who follow the Stations of the Cross gain comfort from it. I decided to reflect on the fourteen stations as an archetypal journey reflecting the struggles and the paradoxes of being human. I designed fourteen cloth-covered panels and incorporated old tools, bark, and branches scavenged from our New England landscape. Layers of change and loss were embedded in these objects. The wall panels followed my own journey from its beginning in "voicelessness," through loss, fear, and doubt, ultimately through a doorway to understanding. I exhibited the fourteen panels as *Stations of the Heart*.

After *Stations of the Heart*, I was ready for a project that didn't involve anything that was old, rusty, heavy, or needed to be welded. I wanted a new medium. Following the suggestion of a friend, sculptor Nancy Schon, I ordered ten pounds of wax from the Reed Wax Company. I put a large chunk in an enamel turkey roaster and clamped a light to the pan to melt the wax enough to make it malleable. In college, I had sculpted the human figure, taking classes at neighboring Haverford College while I was an art major at Bryn Mawr College. Bryn Mawr only had one art professor who taught printmaking, so anyone who wanted to major in art also studied at Haverford. It was a traditional department, and almost every course offered was either sculpting in clay or painting from the live model. With my new wax, it seemed natural to start making small figures, that's what my fingers knew how to do. I would then take the finished figures and place them all over my studio—on an old wheel, inside a tree trunk or hanging from some old tool. I loved giving these small figures their own worlds to inhabit. When I had a collection of waxes, I took them to the foundry that Nancy had suggested and had them cast into bronze. I sold these sculptures as soon as they were finished.

Then the monastery announced an art assignment. Twice a year the entire Zen community studies a Buddhist text. Not only do we study it with our mind, but we explore it through art. I loved this challenge. Even though I was only a beginning Zen student, I decided to create a version of *The Ox Herding Journey*, the Zen Buddhist series that had led me to the monastery. What is this ox? What are the stages of the spiritual path? What is meant by the words "realizing one's true nature"? I didn't have a clue. I looked up ox herding images on the internet, but I could only find versions that were painted or drawn. No three-dimensional sculptures. *Could I render the series as sculptures?*

I made a woodcutter kneeling beside a tree stump, his small saw leaning on the trunk and accompanied the sculpture with the words

Alone and exhausted, you begin your search. Then I needed to make *Finding Traces of the Ox.* In the ink drawing, the traces are tracks of the ox letting the seeker know he is on the right path. I made three tiny oxen, each one smaller than the next, and two mountains creating a scene with the woodcutter on his hands and knees following the oxen deep into the mountains.

The woodcutter finally finds the ox and is able to toss his rope around its thick neck. The ox fights back. The ox is stubborn and strong. Eventually, with persistence and gentleness, the woodcutter is able to tame the ox. At first they walk together tethered by the rope, but as trust builds, they stroll side by side, the tether gone. The woodcutter eventually returns home, sitting on the back of the ox, playing a flute. I made each of these stages as its own sculpture. In the final stage, the seeker *Enters the Marketplace*, returning to daily life, ready to offer help wherever he is needed, while no trace of the journey remains. In actuality, to go through these stages takes decades of practice. The ox in the parable is none other than our stubborn mind, more difficult to train than any animal.

When I brought my ten sculptures to the monastery for the evening presentation of our art practice, I saw my teacher peering at my small figures, but he never said anything. That's the way of Zen training. The teacher knows, and I would learn too, the journey never ends. My understanding would grow and change. There was no need to tell me if what I had done was right or wrong. I was exploring in my own way, and he knew to trust the practice.

A few months later, I exhibited both *The Stations of the Heart* and *The Ox Herding Series* at Andover Newton Theological School in Newton, Massachusetts. Five years later, I would explore ox herding again in sculpture. This time I made larger sculptures, and this time, the seeker was a woman. I even made the ox with udders.

Still fascinated with the idea of a spiritual map, I asked Fruitlands if they would like a labyrinth. The director, Maud Ayson, thought it was a great idea, and I worked with the curator of collections, Mike Volmar, to find a location for a large stone labyrinth on the museum grounds. Fruitlands would pay for the stones, and I'd map out the path and gather enough friends to build it. The curator called me excitedly a few days later and said, "Linda, there's a Pima basket in the collections, it's called *Man in a Maze*." I explained the difference between a labyrinth and maze. "Mazes have false turns and dead ends, and to find the center usually involves retracing one's steps and starting over. A labyrinth is a continuous journey, a winding path with no wrong turns, no wrong decisions. Can you send me a photo?"

He sent me a photo of *Man in a Maze*, a basket by the Akimei O'odham (Pima) people of Arizona. Although the basket was called *Man in a Maze*, the design was actually a labyrinth. The pattern was similar to a traditional Celtic pattern where the labyrinth leads us almost exactly to the center. But then, we are turned away and must go all the way back out to the edge. We continue walking around and around, spiraling inwards until we arrive for a second time at the center. But still, there is no opening to access the center space. It's disappointing. The path leads us back to the beginning. Then, with one last turn, we find ourselves walking directly into the center. The irony is that once we arrive, the space is empty. We find only what meaning we give it. After a pause, we resume our walking and follow the winding way back out.

The return journey, however, feels different. We are less worried about arriving somewhere. Walking a labyrinth teaches us to take our steps with consciousness. We feel the earth with each step. We connect. Our breathing quiets. As we continue to practice walking the labyrinth, we learn to forget the coming and going, we just walk. Walking a labyrinth is a walking meditation. We walk, we follow the path one step at a time wherever it leads, and we realize with each step, that's where we are.

Five years later, Fruitlands decided to remove the labyrinth. They kindly offered to drop off the stones at Old Frog Pond Farm. I thought someday I'd rebuild it. You can still see the basket in Fruitlands' collections. Its fine weave expresses stillness and balance, qualities walking a labyrinth restores. You can even walk the labyrinth basket by slowly following the pattern with your finger.

Drawing and sculpture weren't the only arts emerging at the farm. Susan Edwards Richmond, the woman I met during our first season of raspberry picking, and I had become friends. We both had articles written about us in the arts and culture newspaper *The Middlesex Beat* by poet Terry House. Susan had published her first book of poetry, *Boto*, inspired by stories of a pink dolphin called Boto by the indigenous people who live along the Amazon River. The paper was also reviewing *Winter Air*, a letterpress book with digital prints, short prose, and haiku poems that I created as a memorial to my mother. The *Beat's* editor had said to me, "You and Susan must meet." We did, and from that first meeting, came years of creative projects. We co-founded with two other friends *Wild Apples: a journal of nature, art, and inquiry*. We taught writing workshops once a week for inmates at the Shirley Medium Security prison and produced a chapbook of their poetry. In his preface, Jimmy Santiago Baca wrote, ". . . these poems strike at the heart of ignorance and inform us of one important factor—that behind the bars and walls of America's prisons be the pens and papers: behind the judges and lawyers and probation officers and cops and correctional therapists are human beings with dreams and hopes and loves and lives."

When I introduced Susan to Fruitlands Museum, Maud asked her to be their first "Poet-in-Residence." Susan wrote a collection of poems, *Increase*, inspired by the Shakers rejection of worldly concerns and intentions to live isolated in spiritual community. She also organized a *Plein Air Poetry* event with other poets. Each poet was to visit Fruitlands, choose an artifact or feature of the landscape that inspired him or her, and write a poem. They gathered one summer afternoon and shared their poems. The following year when the museum declined to continue with *Plein Air Poetry*, I suggested Susan bring it to the farm. Now in its eighth year, our Old Frog Pond Farm stable of poets continues to grow. We've had to invest in a portable sound system to amplify the voice of the poet so everyone can hear.

With Susan and the other poets and artists, the farm with its diversity of habitats, woods, pond, orchard, and fields, had become an oasis for the arts. For our annual sculpture exhibit openings, musicians gather and play throughout the afternoon. Their music echoes over the pond and can be heard by the apple pickers as well as visitors walking the trails. Blase always brings out his African drum for a few songs. At a performance by Steven Collins celebrating the poetry and life of Walt Whitman, the audience watched an aging Whitman (Steven has a remarkable resemblance to him) open his arms, embrace the immeasurable sky, and exclaim:

> Love the earth and sun and the animals, despise riches,
> give alms to everyone that asks, stand up for the stupid
> and crazy, devote your income and labor to others . . .
> re-examine all you have been told at school or church
> or in any book, dismiss whatever insults your own soul . . . . 🌱

Row 19: Vows

I often carry a loupe with me into the orchard, a small eyepiece that magnifies fifteen times. It helps to identify the stages of an insect's life cycle. Ladybugs, for example, begin their lives as tiny clusters of yellow eggs on the underside of a leaf. After they hatch, they grow into larvae with long tails like miniature alligators with nothing to suggest their familiar spotted shell.

Ladybugs are beneficial to the orchard. They eat aphids, sap-sucking insects that begin their lives as gray and brown egg clusters on the underside of leaves. When the aphids mature, they venture forth and destroy the newest green shoots on a tree, sucking out the juice from the underside until there is nothing left but the leaf fiber. They go where the food is most tender and fresh to find the nutrients they need. On large trees they aren't a problem, but on the small ones they can colonize every new shoot, and the tree loses a year of growth.

When I looked at a mass of aphids with the loupe, they looked like a horrific congregation of engorged ticks. When I looked at my hand with the loupe, I was shocked. My skin was pocked and scaly, strange and

Shuso *ceremony, 2021*   *Photo: Zen Mountain Monastery*

otherworldly, like an alien hand in a science fiction movie. It was the same skin I always saw, but I had never seen it magnified.

Gazing at my hand reminded me of a childhood experience. When I was about six years old, I walked into the alley behind our small row house, carrying a metal kitchen bowl. It was the insert from the classic Revere Ware double boiler. Then, seating myself in a patch of weeds, I gathered the long stalks that grew in abundance. I rubbed my fingers up the stem against the grain and the seeds fell off, accumulating in the pot. Then, a most pleasurable experience ensued: I traced my fingers through the bowl of seeds. In that touching, I was complete and the world was whole. The weed, I discovered later, was plantain, and when I see it growing in the orchard I occasionally reach down, pluck a stem, and rub the seeds off from the stalk.

Since then I've learned that plantain is a beneficial plant for insect bites. Though I had to go to the hospital when I inadvertently blocked the entrance to a large nest of white-faced hornets, receiving multiple stings on my face and neck, my body has adapted to the occasional sting of a honeybee. When I am stung, I pick a few plantain leaves, chew them well, and use them as a poultice. The plantain along with resting my body and drinking lots of water means I don't have to use an Epi-pen. Ever since that experience with the white-faced hornets, I am careful walking among the trees in late summer, always on the lookout for their round paper nests.

When I saw the upper half of a good sized apple tree had no leaves, I panicked. *What could be wrong?* Then I saw it—a six-inch caterpillar, emerald green. On its head was an arrangement of yellow knobs with protruding black hairs, its body spiraled with smaller blue knobs. My hand shot up to grab the beast. Get this leaf-eating monster out of the orchard. Its mouth looked like Jabba the Hutt, with folds of flesh hiding a rapacious opening. I gently touched its tender belly with my fingertips, then grabbed and tugged, but its legs clung fiercely to the branch. I couldn't pull it off or its innards, the guts . . . it would be too gruesome.

I went to get loppers to remove the branch. On the way back to the orchard I stopped at the house to look up what I had seen. It was easy to identify—a Cecropia caterpillar. I bookmarked the page, returned to the tree, and cut off the branch.

Carrying the branch with the caterpillar, I thought, *What if the new home I choose for it isn't safe? What will it eat?* I started to worry about what I had done. Later I read more about the Cecropia life cycle. It takes a full year from larva to moth. This caterpillar was poised to become the largest silk moth in North America. The caterpillar had been a rare gift, and I had responded too quickly. I've never seen another Cecropia caterpillar though my eyes are trained to look for bare branches.

In early August, a denuded branch in the orchard is a sign the red-humped caterpillars have arrived. These red-and-gold-striped caterpillars appear in masses in the tops of trees. How they get there I don't know, but eating the leaves, they work their way down the branches, growing fatter every day. I don't spray the orchard in order to get rid of them. Just like the aphids, a few clusters of red-humped caterpillars in the mature trees don't matter. The tiny caterpillars will grow into thick ones, and the birds eventually will pick them off. But left on a young tree, every leaf will be eaten in a couple of days. I need to be vigilant and find and pick off any masses in the young trees.

I returned to Zen Mountain Monastery for weekend retreats every couple of months. On the four-hour drive over to the Catskills, I would leave behind the responsibilities of the farm. Blase was there and he would look after Ariel who was the only one of our children living at home. After completing a retreat on the Buddhist precepts, I felt ready to take my Buddhist vows. They signify a commitment to live one's life with compassion for all sentient beings, to practice good, to not cause harm. The precepts in Buddhism are not hard and fast rules, but intentions about a way to live. After all, I was killing sentient beings each time I picked off a caterpillar or a Japanese beetle. But I was starting to see that every decision I made, every action had an effect. I would never forget Daido Roshi's passionate pronouncement, "You are responsible for the whole catastrophe."

During the week before the taking-the-vows ceremony, the student lives at the monastery and sews a *rakusu*, a black bib-like cloth, chanting her vows with every stitch. The *rakusu* is made up many small pieces all sewn together. It is the lay practitioner's version of the *kesa*, the saffron-colored robe the Buddha and his monastic community wore. The tradition goes back to a time in India even before the Buddha. When a person left home to become a mendicant he would sew a garment using cloth taken from corpses before their cremation and dye it yellow. This would be his only clothing, all else was left behind. The Buddha continued the custom by having those who wanted to join his community sew their own robe from discarded cloth.

Every day after early morning meditation, Zen students around the world recite the *Verse of the Kesa*. While reciting these lines, the practitioner places the folded rakusu they have sewn on their head and recites the verse twice. They then unfold it and wear it for the last recitation.

> Vast is the robe of liberation,
> A formless field of benefaction.
> I wear the Tathagata's teaching,
> Saving all sentient beings.

The Tathagata is a Sanskrit word that refers to Shakyamuni Buddha. The formless field of benefaction is a place where one feels joy and peace. And the last line is the quite impossible vow to save all beings in the world. It's impossible, yet we vow to do it every day.

Before the ceremony, the student gives their *rakusu* to their teacher who writes on the inside of it the Dharma name he has chosen for that student. My teacher gave me the name *Shinji*. Shin in Japanese means truth or reality; Ji means earth, soil, or ground. He told me the name meant "Earth Reality," but it could also be "Truth in the Soil." One's Buddhist name becomes a teaching to contemplate, a traveling companion for life. I wear my *rakusu* whenever I meditate, a physical reminder of my vows. When I'm not sitting, my *rakusu* is folded neatly inside the black-and-white leaf scarf that held my mother's ashes on the trip to

Pspua New Guinea.

"Truth is in Soil" is literally what I have been learning from growing apples. The region around the root system is a highly complex network of interrelationships: of fungi, bacteria, and mycelium which all live together. It is one of the densest communities of living creatures in the world. Here are the populations of soil farmers who nourish the plant world. We eat because of the diversity of microbes on the earth, because of this "Truth in the Soil."

A recent study of healthy plants grown in biologically rich soil proved that ninety percent of all nutrients absorbed by plants were once part of soil organisms. Plants grown in dysfunctional soils need chemical fertilizers. Most soils in America no longer have healthy biological activity. We need to do everything we can to encourage these microorganisms. Saving all sentient beings makes good sense.

Another Japanese farmer's approach caught my attention. Masanobu Fukuoka (1913–2008) was also determined to farm without using chemical pesticides. His book *One Straw Revolution*, published in English in 1978, became an underground manifesto for farmers seeking a new approach to agriculture, one that did no harm and was not dependent on chemicals. He wanted a way to farm that was truly in harmony with nature.

He railed against the modern methods of using chemicals, new practices that were introduced in Japan after World War II. At first these chemicals meant less work for the farmers, but it took only one generation before the healthy soil was depleted, and the crops became dependent on synthetic fertilizers and pesticides.

Fukuoka is best known for his radically new approach to growing rice. I was most interested in how Fukuoka created an orchard of clementines on a clay hillside above his family's farm. "The red clay was so hard you could not stick a shovel into it," he wrote. People had grown potatoes here, exhausted the soil, and abandoned the fields. He knew he had to build up the organic matter to restore the soil before anything would grow. First he dug holes and added organic materials, a physically demanding effort that led nowhere. He buried straw and ferns he carried on his back from high up on the mountain. But portaging ninety pounds and digging trenches was exhausting, and the trenches caved in as the plant material settled. He then thought of burying wood that would decompose more slowly but it wasn't available nearby. He arrived at his *aha* moment—he would grow the wood himself.

Among the citrus trees already growing, he planted pine, cedar, pear, loquat, cherry, and other native trees. On the bare ground under them he sowed white clover and alfalfa. The clover grew and blanketed the hillside. He planted daikon, the large white Japanese radish. With its deep taproot, the daikon opened the way for water and air to circulate through the hard clay. The radish reseeded, softening the clay soil, and, after a few seasons, Fukuoka could plant root crops like potatoes and eventually more tender vegetables. He continued to sow clover, a nitrogen-fixing plant that returned more nitrogen to the soil than it used. His orchard soil became rich and dark, and the tall trees provided a windbreak protecting the smaller citrus trees.

Inspired by Fukuoka, I ordered comfrey plants for the orchard. Like the daikon radish, comfrey has a long tap root and will go down like a miner to bring minerals up to the topsoil. Gardeners know comfrey spreads from its seeds like a weed and will take over a garden. I ordered Russian comfrey because it is self-sterile and propagates only from a root cutting. I needn't have worried; deer browsed the plants back to the ground. They slowly regrew and I was grateful they were at least alive, but I realized they would never flourish in the orchard unless I had irrigation. The soil in the orchad wasn't clay—quite the opposite. It was rocky, fast-draining soil. Even though we were on the map for growing organic apples, I knew our soils were poor and nothing like the loamy, rich soils I was reading about.

I wanted to follow the way of natural farming and imagined our orchard filled with clover and wildflowers. We would still need to keep the aisles clear for the tractor, but I could fill all the spaces between the trees with beneficial herbs and flowers. I aspired to Fukuoka's ease and trust of nature. I felt connected to these orchardists in Japan. I wasn't sure what I was going to do, but for several weeks I carried Fukuoka's book in my back pocket so his spirit would infuse the farm. ❦

Orchard Earth

Now the buds begin to break. The firm winter-buds swell. Their scales part. Tips of green appear. Tiny leaves come forth, neatly rolled inward, growing as they expand, the stalks lengthening. Resurrection is astir in the tree.

—Liberty Hyde Bailey

Row 20: Naked to the Core

In 2011, ten years after moving to the farm, undressing in front of a mirror, my eye fell upon the nipple on my left breast. The nipple was slightly inverted. With two fingers I tried to pull it out, but something had a firm grip. That's when I felt a lump about three-quarters of an inch across, the size of an apple in July.

I went to see my general practitioner who sent me for a mammogram and an ultrasound, and scribbled down the names of two surgeons. I didn't pay much attention to the names. *I probably wouldn't need them.*

"Undress from the waist up. Tie the Johnny in front."

The technician wedged my small breast under two plates of plastic. "Hold your breath," she said. Then pulled a lever to flatten the breast. After the mammogram, she took an ultrasound image.

I took a seat in a room with other women waiting for imaging results. Glancing at the stack of magazines, *People*, *Entertainment*, and *House and Garden*, I saw a copy of a newsletter from the *Union of Concerned Scientists*. On the cover was a short feature on Monsanto titled, "Agribusiness giant Monsanto has a serious image problem." It turned out

Haircutting with daughter, Ariel, 2011

that Roundup, their flagship weed killer, was so overused that, "Round-up-ready weeds infested an area of United States farmland roughly equal to the state of Michigan." Superweeds, they were called.

Even scarier, scientific data showed the active ingredient, glyphosate, was carcinogenic, but Roundup remains on the shelves of every box store in the country, and the company disputes the findings despite having to pay millions of dollars in lost lawsuits.

The nurse called my name and I entered the doctor's cave where a desk curved around three-quarters of the room, and on the wall were four computer screens. Each one displayed my breast enlarged maybe a hundred times. The mammogram showed normal breast tissue, but the ultrasound revealed an amorphous matter, a jellyfish about four centimeters wide splayed over the front of the breast. Over the last five years, my mammograms had shown I have dense breast tissue. What I didn't know was that a tumor the size of a mature apple would not show up on mammograms for this group of women. One in ten women have dense breast tissue making it even more important for them to do regular self-exams. The radiologist wrote down the names of two surgeons. One was a familiar name; the same name my general practitioner had given me. The doctor advised the first step was to have a core biopsy of the mass taken.

I take soil samples in the orchard every spring using a thin spade. These I send out to a lab to determine the balance of minerals in the soil. Health of the soil determines health of the tree. Health of the tree determines health of the food. Two days later I walked into a sterile room fully occupied by an examination table and a bright metal machine with a monitor. A doctor directed several hollow needles through my breast and into the solid mass to remove core samples. A few days later the tests came back positive.

I went with Blase to talk with the surgeon. "We'll do a sentinel node biopsy to determine whether the cancer has spread to the lymph nodes under your arm."

"How do you do that?" I asked.

While quickly sketching on a scrap of paper, she explained, "I make an incision, cut through some nerves and muscle, and remove a few lymph nodes. They are sent to the lab and if they show cancer, then we assume that cells have spread throughout your body."

I thought of botanists who discovered that trees share nutrients with other trees. After injecting radioisotopes into one tree, they watched as the radioactive material flowed down into the roots and up into the trunk of a neighboring tree. Scientists have even seen nutrients flow from a dying tree to a tree of another species which needs the boost. I was determined not to be on a battlefield. Hadn't I been in the orchard enough to notice how nature finds balance? An infestation of caterpillars brings birds to eat them. Aphids provide food for ladybugs. Braconid wasps eat apple maggot flies. Michael Phillips says the richer the diversity in the orchard, the more natural allies we have. Where were my friends? What was happening in my body?

In the surgeon's office I was on a battlefield: if this, then that; if not that, then this. She was writing down orders for a battery of tests I would need prior to surgery: PET scan, CAT scan, MRI, blood work, lung scan. I wondered why a lumpectomy and not a full mastectomy? The surgeon was going too fast for me.

She also wanted me to see an oncologist. Blase and I went see Dr. J., a slight man with curling brown hair who wore a long white lab coat. "I want to get you well and back to your life," he said. That was good to hear. There was a barrage of details to assimilate. What kind of cancer did I have? How aggressive was it? What stage was I at? Would I need chemotherapy? Radiation?

Dr. J. patiently answered every question. He'd been through this type of interrogation hundreds of times before, but his patience felt infinite. He made sure we understood what we wanted to know. I told him I felt rushed by the surgeon and would like to speak to another. He said, "I always welcome second opinions." His office would help me make the appointment.

Blase and I went to see a surgeon at the Faulkner Breast Center in

Boston for our second opinion. The center had been founded in the 1960s by Dr. Susan Love, a pioneer in treating women with breast cancer. In a flowing brown dress, Dr. M. conveyed regal authority. We followed her into a tiny office. Although she was the director of this prominent breast center, no leather chairs or large mahogany desk announced her importance, only the barest of essentials: a pad of blank paper, a few pencils, and a small computer screen off to the side. The visit didn't take long; she looked over the tests. "Yes, we can do a mastectomy and lymph node biopsy at the same time."

One surgery. It was not a battleground; it was surgery to remove a problem. In the orchard, when there is a branch infected by fire blight, we immediately cut and burn. Quick removal prevents the bacterium from infecting the entire tree. I could understand surgery; I was not afraid of losing a breast. I was in a relationship I expected to be in for the rest of my life. Cut off my breast and give me back my life.

The surgery was set for July 8. By some miracle, before this diagnosis, we had rented a house on Cape Cod for two weeks in the middle of June. I had planned to go back and forth, a two-hour drive, work in the orchard and relax at the Cape. Instead, with this diagnosis, I decided to spend as much time as possible by the ocean. My son Nick was between seasons of work, and he came with me. Blase needed to stay at the farm and would come down on weekends. Ariel, though living at the farm, was working at a horse stable seven days a week. Alex lived in North Carolina, an apprentice to Matt Jones, a potter trained in the wood-fired traditions of both Asian and English pottery.

The house was on one of the kettle ponds in Wellfleet. If the wind was in the right direction, we could hear the sound of the surf from across the dunes. A short walk around the pond on a wooded trail and we arrived at a deserted beach. The vacationers with school-age children would not arrive until the end of June. I walked for miles on that beach, watching the waves and listening to the cries of gulls and terns playing in the updrafts. The seals popped up here and there offshore, interrogating with their doglike gazes. A tanker made its way slowly across the

horizon. The beach changed every day, every moment, yet it was trust-
worthy. I wanted to be able to trust my body.

On the weekend, Nick and Blase fished for bluefish and striper. They
stood on the beach, casting their baited lines, but the seals scared away
the fish. After hours of reeling in empty lures, Nick decided to take
a kayak out beyond the seals. Blase and I watched as he disappeared.
An hour passed, during which I imagined I saw him several times bob-
bing in the waves, but no, it was always a lobster pot. Another hour
went by. He had no drinking water and no life vest. My thoughts raced
with the possibility of his disappearance; our eyes were glued to the
ocean. I turned to Blase, "What do we do? Call the Coast Guard?" In
my mind, I had already called the Coast Guard many times. Blase just
said, "Wait." We continued to watch the horizon.

I knew Nick would be furious if I made a scene, but he could also be
in dire straits. How could I sit by and not save my son from sharks and
the undertow, dehydration, and disorientation? It might already be too
late. He could be miles out. What would I say to his father?

After what seemed an eternity, we saw him on his way back to shore.
He pulled his small kayak onto the beach. A large bluefish covered the
bow and a crowd gathered. He told us he'd thrown back seven other
blues and hung out with a pod of whales. I kept quiet, but when he
announced the next day he'd be going out again, I handed him a life
jacket; he already had a liter of water.

When we returned home I checked the orchard. Golf ball-sized
green apples hung on the branches. It looked like a decent crop, though
the young trees we had planted in April were clearly struggling. They
hadn't been watered and needed weeding, but the surgery was upper-
most in my mind. The night before my operation, I asked Nick and
Ariel if they wanted to write a message to the surgeon. Nick acted like
this was the most normal request in the world. I got a black permanent
marker, handed it to him, and pulled my shirt down modestly so the
top of my breast showed. He wrote, "Not just any breast. This is my
mother."

Ariel added, "Please, be careful. Thank you."

Two weeks after surgery, I saw my surgeon for a checkup. She said the incision was healing well and asked about my next steps. I told her I was seeing Dr. J. and evaluating whether or not to do chemotherapy.

"You need to have chemotherapy." In her look of horror, I read, *It would be a waste of surgery not to have it.*

Like the invasive plants on the farm, I knew the entire tumor had to be removed or it would return. To stop the spread, it's necessary to get every single cancer cell out of the body. But in the orchard I had made the commitment not to use chemicals, no matter what the pest or invasive plant I encountered. I was trying so hard to find a natural way to grow fruit, a way of being on the earth that didn't cause harm. Now I was being asked if I wanted to use chemicals in my body.

Blase and I went to see my oncologist again. Dr. J. gave us data from decades of women with my kind of cancer. Pages of numbers and outlines accumulated in my lap. The statistics recommended a three-month protocol of chemotherapy.

A friend wanted me to check out a holistic cancer treatment center in Texas. "I would never use chemotherapy," she said vehemently. Others had other ideas. But Dr. J. had made his recommendations clear. It was my body and my decision. In Zen we say, *you have to take your seat.* You have to sit on your meditation cushion and examine your mind. I was sitting in a murky pond, waiting for the particles to settle.

When my mother received her cancer diagnosis, she was given six months to live. After one round of chemotherapy and an aborted second round, Anna's oncologist in New York said he could do nothing further. That's when she took over. She traveled to Budapest for some special vials. She went to Tijuana where an American doctor, by coincidence, the brother of her New York oncologist, was experimenting with large doses of vitamins to pump up the immune systems of his patients. These injections, not sanctioned by the Food and Drug Administration, were secretly given at night in an empty warehouse.

Anna tried coffee enemas, vitamins from Canada—any and every suggestion that offered hope. The most unconventional treatment she received was a healing technique described in the Talmud and practiced for over two thousand years by Hasidic Jews. Anna went with one of her close friends to a small room in New Jersey where an elderly man covered her with a white sheet, except for a small hole cut in the material to reveal her belly. The man held a pigeon firmly against her skin. The pigeon started to breathe with difficulty, then choke, cough, and sputter, until it fell over and died, presumably from the toxins it had absorbed. The man then placed another pigeon on her belly, and another, until seven pigeons had died. It's hard to believe this sequence of events really happened, that the doctor wasn't some charlatan performing quack voodoo, and secretly strangling the birds, but Anna told me it was the truth.

Whether due to all of the alternative remedies or simply due to her strong desire to fight her illness, Anna lived for three years after her initial diagnosis, much longer than the six months she had been given. I was not prompted to seek alternatives with my mother's degree of desperation. We all have different responses when faced with choices for our health and mortality. Maybe I was in denial. I couldn't see my cancer cells. I resisted the label of breast cancer and only referred to "my diagnosis." At the monastery, people who are ill are put on a health and healing list. I didn't want to hear my name chanted along with the others who were ill. *May they heal all their ills and may we attain the Buddha way together.* I didn't want to be labeled as sick.

Sometimes in the orchard I have to decide whether a sick or injured tree has enough strength and health to be saved, or if it is better to cut it down and replant. I've kept a damaged tree for several years only to watch its slow demise and have to take it out anyway. Other times I give the sick tree extra compost, more minerals, and nutrient sprays, and it revives.

I decided to visit the monastery before I gave Dr. J. my answer about treatment. On my drive, I stopped in a rest area bathroom. A colorful poster on the wall warned people to dispose of medications properly: *Pills are poisoning our water supply.* In addition to the painkillers, antidepressants, and antibiotics that are flushed down the toilet, our bodies excrete small amounts of the medications we take. Of particular concern are the endocrine disruptors, similar to how glyphosate in Roundup disrupts the growth of weeds. It wasn't only herbicides and pesticides poisoning the earth, but the plethora of medications people take on a daily basis including chemotherapy drugs. Ironically, the large international pharmaceutical companies like Bayer and DuPont also make fertilizers and pesticides, including the neonicotinoids, the family of chemicals killing the bee population.

At the monastery I was grateful to be assigned a room to myself rather than the usual bunkroom with six or eight other women. Early the next morning the bell rang, and we all walked in silence into the *zendo*, the meditation hall. Sitting in the quiet of the *zendo*, feelings from the last few months rose: the nightmares I had pushed away—fear of dying, fear of my children losing their mother, sadness at not being able to meet my grandchildren, leaving this earth, this planet, the trees, the farm. Loud crying during group meditation happens only occasionally, usually the *zendo* is silent except for the occasional cough or sneeze. But when I thought of my children, my body simply convulsed with loud weeping. I tried to be still, for in Zen we do not move, we do not sniff our nose or rub away tears, we just wait in the stillness until the bell sounds to end the sitting period. A steady stream fell from my nose and tears dripped down my face, my chin, and onto my *rakusu*. I tried not to attach to any one thought, but to let them go, and return to just sitting, but my sobbing continued. At home I had tried to be strong, and had held in my tears. Now my body released its own expressive oratorio.

Gradually, though, as a child exhausts her crying, the panic I had allowed myself to feel lessened. Something shifted. The darkness of early morning turned into dawn, and the mourning doves outside the window started cooing. Whether I was calm or crying, fearful, or content, there was only sitting. When my mind stopped thinking, just this sitting.

Breakfast followed meditation, and the bell sounded for work practice. I expected something easy; of course they wouldn't assign me to shovel compost or carry wood. I imagined sewing or plant care. I loved work practice and always found it to be one of the most instructive activities for watching my mind. In the silence of work practice, I could catch myself thinking of a better way to do a task, or notice how easily I shifted from being attentive to daydreaming. I heard my name called and the assignment "personal care." It felt odd; I'd never heard this assigned as a practice. I went back to my room, lay down, and fell deeply asleep. My body needed rest. I had no trouble with this caretaking.

I sat with my teacher at a picnic table over lunch. "I hate the idea of injecting chemicals. What would you do?" He offered no Buddhist theory, no Zen teachings. He didn't bring up our vows to save all sentient beings. He didn't talk about ecology or the earth. He looked at me and said, "I would do anything. I would try everything offered."

He never asked what I was going to do, but before we got up, he said, "Please take this with you." It was a tiny walnut box.

"It holds colored sand from a sand painting, a mandala created by Tibetan monks."

I put the box in my pocket, we hugged, and I packed for home.

※

Mandala paintings are geometric depictions of a Buddhist teaching about the universe. All over Asia, mandalas are painted in temples and shrines, on mud walls, on wood, or on cloth. Usually the artist begins with a central subject, a goddess or a Buddha, then surrounds this main figure with other gods, animals, trees, or mountains, or the elements of earth, water, fire, and air. Whatever the subject, the mandala is a work of pattern, color, repetition, and variation. It's not a representation of a scene—it's an energetic visual prayer, an appreciation of the healing power of the chosen deity or a portal to connect with them. In the case of a sand mandala, when it is complete, the image is brushed away. The gathered grains of sand are returned to a flowing river—a reminder of the impermanence of all things. My teacher told me he had kept this memento of impermanence on his altar for more than twenty years. I felt his love and was grateful. I didn't open it to look inside until I got home, but when I did, it was empty; the sand had somehow disappeared.

At home, I told Blase about my visit. He was silent, respectful of my process. We never talked about his fear of losing me. We didn't discuss that possibility. The compelling documentation from Dr. J. along with my teacher's response made my decision simple. I recognized how fortunate I was to have the opportunity to do something to stop the growth of cancer cells. I approached chemotherapy as yet another mountain to climb. I was ready to lose my hair.

I'd worn my thick, dark, waist-length hair in a long braid since I was twelve years old. However, in my late forties, it started to turn gray, and I began to color it. As the years went by I felt disgusted that I was dyeing it. It felt inauthentic. Stopping, however, was difficult, since it would literally take years to grow out. When I mentioned to Blase I wanted to stop using hair color, he laughed and said, "Oh, you'll look like a skunk."

Now the question of hair color was moot. A few nights before treatment was to begin, I put my hair in two braids, each one more than twenty inches long. Ariel and I had already discussed the hair issue. She told me the organization Locks of Love takes donations of hair to make wigs for people undergoing chemotherapy. Ariel had decided in solidarity she would cut her own long hair and send it to them as well. When my haircutting time came, I gave Ariel a pair of scissors. She cut off one of my braids, then Blase cut off the other one. After a lifetime of long hair, I now had short hair. One of my braids went to Locks of Love. Blase put the other on his altar in our bedroom. This haircutting was empowering and freeing. I was ready for change.

After two treatments my short hair started falling out, and I asked Blase to shave my head. He massaged thick shaving cream from a tube into my scalp before he began with the razor. The raspy sound as razor scraped against scalp reminded me of pulling the pruned apple branches out from under the winter trees. Then Blase wiped my bald head with a warm, wet washcloth—his touch, a most intimate caring.

Some ritual purification was happening, and it felt curiously familiar. The monks at the monastery shave their heads every week, and I was used to seeing both men and women with no hair on their heads. Hair loss for women takes away their identity, but for me it reinforced my connection with the teachings of Zen and the monastery. I was bald like some of the women I most admired.

Hair is such a defining physical feature. Our style, our age, our desire to conform or to be different. Watching people run their hands through their hair or tangle a strand around a finger can show comfort or discomfort. Having no hair was a welcome and freeing change, except when I was out doing errands. Shopping at the supermarket or picking up something at the local hardware store, I didn't want to draw attention to myself or to my diagnosis.

When I parked at a local produce store, I leaned over to grab a hat, and the woman in the car next to mine rolled down her window. As I turned to look she smiled and began taking off her wig. We chatted for a few minutes. She told me she had ovarian cancer and said, "I can't stand wearing a wig, but my grown children prefer it." Though we were strangers a deep bond of understanding connected us.

At my next appointment with Dr. J. he looked at me and said, "Linda, you could get a wig, you know." I shook my head.

"Well," he said, "you're lucky. You have a nicely-shaped head."

At home I had a routine, a station on the red leather sofa in the living room. The first days after a treatment were always the worst. I was feverish, achy, and dizzy. But after a week, I was on the mend, and by day ten, I was starting to feel quite good. On day fourteen, when I was almost back to normal, I would go in for the next treatment.

Blase fed me bowls of home-grown kale sautéed in olive oil with garlic and soy sauce, and I drank lots of our own nettle mint tea. Ariel had suggested I read the Harry Potter series. I escaped to this magical world by day, but at night I had dreams of peril. In one, I was lost without a wallet, without money, and without identification. I couldn't find my way home. In a variation, I was driving Nick's motorcycle, and it was out of gas. I had no money to fill it up, and my cell phone was out of juice. I couldn't get home. I didn't know where I was.

In the most disturbing dream, I was lying on a hospital bed looking down at my hip, but I only saw a tiny piece of bone. Then I realized my pelvis was a fan of fragile bird bones in the flattened shape of a gentle waterfall. When I reached down to the foot of the bed for a paper and pen the bones moved, but I easily set them back in the same pattern. Even though I seemed to be handling this cancer diagnosis well, my dreams revealed my fears. The fragile bones made me realize my vulnerability.

Meanwhile, apple scent filled the orchard and raspberries were ripening on the canes in the patch. Harvest time was here again, and the farm stand needed to open. Nick had stayed through the summer and took over with the help of Blase's son who came up from New York for a few weeks before going to France for a junior year abroad in Paris. A friend arranged for a group of middle school students to help out. Every Saturday and Sunday, students came in pairs for two-hour shifts. Mostly they were on their hands and knees with buckets picking up apple drops, but they also spent time in the kitchen under Nick's supervision, cutting up apples and juicing them for cider.

I ventured out to the stand when I felt well enough. The combination of cancer and organic apples sent the wrong message. I wore a hat, but many customers saw right through it. I forgot that having no eyebrows gave me away. Some pickers spoke quietly about their cancer and asked about mine.

Then, midway through the harvest season, a customer called early on Sunday morning.

"I picked twelve pints of raspberries for jam yesterday, and while I was cooking I noticed small white worms floating on the top of the pot."

"How awful. I'm so sorry. I'll gladly refund your money," I said.

I grabbed my loupe and went out to the patch and picked a few berries. Opening them in the palm of one hand, I peered into the center and saw white squirming larvae inside juicy berries. I didn't need the loupe. A major infestation of something had taken hold throughout the patch.

In 2008, the spotted winged drosophila, an Asian fruit fly, had come from Japan to California and ravaged orchards all along the Pacific coast. It then moved through the Midwest, destroying blueberry crops, and by 2011 it was affecting berry crops all along the East Coast. Usually rotting fruit attracts fruit flies. A bruised pear or peach left on the kitchen counter in summer gathers fruit flies from seemingly nowhere. The spotted winged drosophila, however, is particularly challenging because the female lays eggs in unripe fruit. I trapped a few of the flies and, with my loupe, identified the telltale black spots on the wings. I could see a little curved saw, the ovipositor on the female fly's rear end which she uses to cut into the hard fruit to deposit her eggs. We roped off the patch. At least a thousand pints of raspberries would rot on the canes. It was too late to do anything by the time we discovered the infestation and, anyway, I didn't know what we would do. No one knew how to control this new, invasive pest, especially using organic methods.

The loss for organic California growers in the first year of the spotted winged drosophila appearance was over $500 million. Our loss was $5,000, a small figure in comparison. But, more importantly, raspberries are a wonderful part of our farm's offering. Our upcoming African drumming Sunday afternoon event would not include the festive dancing through the raspberry rows, nor the plucking of berries to the beat of drums.

We have raspberry devotees, people who return again and again to pick throughout the eight-week season. How would we explain it to them? They certainly had consumed some of the white larvae already. When I told a few people, their eyes widened and horror crossed their faces. I decided to just say the patch was *picked out*. We would hopefully have a solution for next year. In the meanwhile, I didn't want people to decide they would never return to pick our raspberries. I put up a rope across the entrance to the patch with a sign: Closed.

The apple crop did well, but when the season ended, I was relieved. I needed to concentrate on my health. ❦

Row 21: October Storm

For my birthday at the end of October, my three children gathered. Blase was away facilitating a weekend men's workshop. On Saturday morning, snow began to fall. All day the snow continued to pile up, and by evening, the tree branches, weighted down by their snow-covered leaves, leaned and fell, knocking out power lines all over New England. The roads were a maze of downed wires and trees. The children and I were in the living room together with two oil lamps for light. We sat in the semi-darkness with no television, movies, or ringing telephones—a rare and magical time.

We didn't talk about cancer; I don't remember even mentioning it. Today, I might know how to talk about it more easily. I would speak about my fear of dying and my love for them, but at the time I didn't know how to begin. I want to believe they understood without my words.

Both Ariel and Alex had flights to catch on Sunday, Ariel to Florida and her professional horse world, and Alex to North Carolina and his pottery. Nick was staying with me until Blase returned. Alex came to the sofa, and I eased myself up as he gave me a hug. I didn't want him to

An infra-red image of the orchard, 2015   Photo: Robert Hesse go. For their entire lives, I had blessed and encouraged my children to go off and be independent, to live their lives and pursue their dreams, the way my mother had always encouraged me. Ariel gave me an awkward hug. She had been hiding her fears. All of the unspoken emotions made these goodbyes excruciatingly difficult. I wanted to wail and throw a tantrum, but I controlled my panic as they picked up their bags.

"Bye, Mama. Bye, Mama."

Blase returned the next day. We had no power for the rest of the week. No running water because the well had an electric pump, no showers, no flushing toilets. Blase kept the house warm with the wood stoves, and we had a few lights at night powered from a small generator. Water we needed came from the pond. For me, it was a long week of introspection. I thought of Anna and her own battle with cancer. I remembered visiting her during one of her hospital stays. I asked, "What was most important in your life?"

She looked at me and replied, "My children."

I never thought I would hear that answer. I was certain it was her work. But now I knew being a mother is the marrow in our bones. I couldn't imagine anything more painful than not being here for my children.

Though still weak I was eager to walk in the orchard after the freak October snowstorm. As I made my way through the rows of apple trees, the damage was alarming. With this unexpected accumulation of weight from the heavy snow, the central leader on many of them had snapped. About thirty trees suffered this setback. Though the damage did not kill the trees, the new growth would take time, and the trees would look disfigured for several years. Hopefully, without other challenges, in time, I would be the only one who knew this chapter of their history.

The first four chemo treatments were manageable, but for the last four, the drug changed, changing everything. One of my drugs, Taxol, is now a chemical formulation, but originally it was an herbal remedy from the bark of old yew trees in the Northwest of the United States. Fierce debates raged between the government and the environmentalists over protecting these ancient trees. The yews grew in isolated pockets of untouched, old-growth forests. The logging world considered them useless, with their irregular twisting trunks. Still, accessing, removing, and shipping the bark for medicine meant destroying large tracts of pristine wilderness. Cancer patients wanted Taxol, and researchers clamored for it. A synthetic alternative was needed. The process of developing one took thirty years from its first discovery to the production of a marketable synthetic version. The yew molecule scientists tried to replicate was actually not one molecule but two, a body and a tail, an odd-shaped one and a shapeshifter that would morph into other patterns. Today, Taxol is a leading cancer-fighting drug. We would never have created this healing medicine in the laboratory without finding it first in nature, and only because these old-growth forests had been protected by their isolation.

I was grateful the synthetic version was saving lives, and the old-growth trees were still growing. Yet, I had an allergic reaction to the Taxol. Hives broke out all over my body. Dr. J. said he could put me in the hospital or I could wait it out. I lay on the red sofa in the living room and cried. I was sicker than I had ever been. I couldn't eat. I couldn't sleep. I itched. I was nauseous, weak, and exhausted. For days I watched closely as everything in the world seemed to slip away. Aside from checking in once a day with the doctor's office, I simply made every effort to forget about my body. When I thought about the toxicity, I was scared. When I could empty my mind, a lightness of being arose. Thoughts of work, relationships, my fears, all disappeared. It was a profound emptying of all ties, yet it left me feeling at peace.

Once the drug had worked its way out of my system, the symptoms subsided. Dr. J. offered me the option to try another synthetic drug, one developed from the European yew. While it functions similarly in killing cancer cells, it has different secondary materials which he believed were the problem. I asked, "Will it change my chances of recurrence significantly?" I'd had five of the eight treatments, and I wanted to be done with them. Dr. J. said he would consult with his colleagues. If he was going to give me another treatment, however, he wanted to begin the following week.

I thought of our rows of Honeycrisp apples. When the trees got to be four or five years old, one by one they snapped off at the root graft. At first I thought it was a disease, some virus in the root or bacteria at the graft, but when my search for a cause led nowhere, I called Adams County Nursery. They told me it was an incompatibility issue with that particular rootstock. The graft wasn't strong; it didn't take well. I was happy the nursery would replace our trees, but I thought of the hundreds of thousands of Honeycrisps on this rootstock that wouldn't survive because of this incompatibility. Seeing our snapped-off trees on the ground, their once vibrant leaves drying to brown in only a day, exposed the fragility of all life.

I didn't have any serious side effects from the new Taxol, but then I had an appointment to see a radiologist. Blase and I sat in a tiny room with the radiation oncology doctor, a large, kindly woman. She asked how I was feeling and then began to explain her recommendation for a course of seven and half weeks of radiation.

"I didn't think I would need radiation after a mastectomy and chemo." I said.

"Your tumor was large, and you have the most aggressive type of breast cancer. And you have lymph node involvement," was the beginning of her list. My hold on the oars of this cancer boat was gone; a fierce storm blew in. I didn't want to have anything to do with her or with radiation. I was done, finished, but she continued a litany of more reasons.

Didn't she know I'd done enough?

"Linda," she said, "If you were my sister, I would go over and shake you and say you have to do this!"

I only wanted to end the cancer journey. Being lost in the wilderness searching for an ox took on new meaning. I had to remember why I was doing all this. This was my life. With her forceful words she was shaking me with kindness. I said *yes* to radiation.

"We like to wait three months between chemo and radiation, until you're stronger."

It was early December. On the winter solstice I would have my last chemotherapy treatment, and radiation would begin in March 2012.

Over Christmas my children returned for a short visit, and throughout January I gained strength. Then, on a crisp cold morning in February, I returned to the orchard, walking slowly down a few rows. I was surprised again by the tree damage. The frayed ends of broken branches and open wounds on the trunk made me squeamish. The trees needed to be cleaned up and the broken branches sawn off with clean cuts. It was time to prune. I phoned Denis and we set up a date for the following week. Pruning together had become our winter ritual. I wouldn't be able to do too much, but I wanted to be with him and at least help prune the young trees. It would be a way to regain some strength and flexibility, and I looked forward to seeing him.

Denis arrived, hopped down from his silver pickup truck, and greeted me with a hug. He looked at the espaliered rows of dwarf apples trees growing near the house and said, "You should be proud. Look at what you've done." The slanting trunks of the dwarf trees created a pattern of diagonal lines eight feet tall and evenly spaced, like the strings on a harp. I could almost hear the Aeolian music. Blase, Denis, and I had grafted these trees in our kitchen a few years earlier with scion wood from Tower Hill's heirloom orchard as well as Nashoba Winery where Denis used to work. I was grateful for his praise. I always saw what I could have done better.

We walked out into the orchard with a layer of fresh snow underfoot. Denis hadn't taken his tools out of his truck, while I carried a pair of loppers. We looked and assessed, the light snow outlined each branch. I pointed out the damage from the October storm. At one point he reached over for my loppers. "Do you mind?" he asked, as he took off a small branch.

"Look at these young trees. They didn't grow at all. No water and no weeding," I said. I'm usually the one who fills the sprayer and waters the trees during dry times. Our rocky soil doesn't hold moisture.

Denis looked, but didn't say a word. The trees were frail, mere twigs sticking out of the snow. We both hoped they would take off next spring.

We looked at the dormant fruit buds on the large trees. "You're going to have a good crop," Denis said. The older trees had deeper roots and were less affected by the summer drought.

Denis got his tools. We began working on a few of the trees together. The small trees were easy. Clip, snip, take off a branch growing toward the center or one too large for the diameter of the trunk. We removed old wood to encourage growth; we lightened the density. Denis was more aggressive about removing wood while I was more reluctant, but overall we seemed to approach a tree with the same intention. As we went for the same branch, our loppers collided and we smiled. ❧

Row 22: Art Practice

It had been many months without any creative work, too many months away from the studio. I was tired from my treatments, and tired of being tired. The canyon separating me from my artistic life seemed impossible to cross. It was time again for the monastery's twice yearly art assignment for the entire community. It would be a perfect way to get myself back into art making. The theme was announced. For the next three months we would all be studying *old age, sickness,* and *death*. The three indisputable facts of human existence, the very realities that had led Siddhartha to leave the palace and take up a spiritual search.

Our assignment was to take the three themes—old age, sickness, and death—and spend one month working with each one, using an art medium of our choice. Not to describe, but to sit with the reality of each of these experiences, to penetrate them as fully as possible, and then express them. My studio was usually a bazaar of small bronze figures, wax figures, hammers, saws, power grinders, drills, found objects, wood, branches, stones, shells, wire, and fibers. The entire space devoted to deconstruction and construction. But given my limited strength, I knew

Source, installation with Margo Stage, 2013

my choice of medium had to be simple. I wasn't going to use power tools or carve wood. Blase and I went to our local consignment store, Tables to Teapots, and bought an old brown sofa so I would have a restful place to sit while in the studio.

On one of my studio walls, a New Guinea fishing net hangs. The net was something Anna had brought back from the Trobriands, and for as long as I could remember, it had hung on the wall in her home office. Made of simple knots and natural fibers, bits of wood, the floaters, are tied along one side, and shells, the sinkers, are tied along the other. I remembered our treks from our inland village to visit coastal villages where we would watch the men fishing in their outrigger canoes along the barrier reef with similar nets.

Anna had taught me to trust the inherent value of cultural arti-facts, the power of these objects as a storehouse for memories as well as currency to use and trade. Inspired by this Trobriand fishing net, I chose string for my medium. High on a studio shelf I had a basket with different sizes of string, rope, and twine. I decided I would learn how to crochet as a first step and went to our local yarn shop and bought the largest crochet hook they had. I found a YouTube video to learn how to do the stitches, but I was disappointed. It wasn't what I had in mind. The process was too organized. I rebelled against the detailed instructions to make even lines and patterns. I wanted a design that was larger, loopier, and less organized. I wanted a process where my brain would not be required to follow such detailed instructions. The little rectangles of crochet I mastered were abysmally pathetic compared to the image I had in mind.

Meanwhile, my hands enjoyed working with the string. Without much forethought, I grabbed a ball of thick twine and began to make loose loops. Following a quiet rhythm, I knotted a loop every ten inches or so. Doing this repetitive work, I let old age permeate my body. A large pile of looped twine accumulated at my feet. When the ball was fin-ished, I picked up the mass by gathering a few of the loops together and hung it from the ceiling. A twined crystal slowly turned, its loops hung chaotically in all directions.

Intrigued, the next day I picked up another ball of twine, this one solid black. I looped for most of the afternoon and then hung up the pile again. This one was smaller and felt different—the black was ominous. While looping, my mind held no ideas of self-expression, no thoughts about the outcome.

The weakness from all the treatments gave me an easy entry to this practice of old age. It was a time of stillness, peace, and serenity. My hands were busy, but I wasn't thinking. My only rule was to finish the ball of rope or twine I started, no matter its length, before taking another ball. The month passed. The dangling masses of looped rope, twine, and yarn hung like strange sea creatures from my ceiling. Some shapes were stiff and short, while others dangled almost to the floor. These sculptures were my "old age" art practice.

The next month I took up the theme of sickness. Sitting on my brown sofa, experiencing sickness, a sense of uselessness took over. A lethargy crept throughout my body. I chose weaker yarns—grays and dull colors. They sagged with nothing to hold them up, no tensile strength like the twine.

During this month of working on sickness I received a request to install two of my old circus sculptures at the Umbrella Center for the Arts in Concord. One of them, *Leon the Lion*, needed a new mane and tail. It had been six years since he had been on exhibit, and his rope mane and tail were bedraggled. I found a vendor for rope and asked the man who answered the phone if he had any short ends he would sell. I couldn't meet the minimum order so he suggested I go on eBay. Disappointed, I started looking online, but within the hour the phone rang. It was the man I had spoken with earlier. "I'd like to send you some pieces of rope if you will send me a photo of *Leon the Lion*."

A box arrived with three sizes of rope: one, two, and three inches thick. Oh, these were magnificent! Something about the purity of the twined fibers touched me, especially the power of the three-inch tug-of-war size, strong enough to keep a cruise boat docked. I repaired the lion and had some left over.

I started experimenting with the one- and two-inch rope. It was harder to manipulate and too stiff for me to make loops. When I untangled its twisted strands they retained the curve of their last incarnation and hung like thick, naturally curly hair. The rope had its own agenda. I couldn't control it. I had found an expression for sickness—surrender, the lesson I had learned from my own diagnosis.

Then the month came to work with death. *I can't do this*, I said to myself. I was finally getting strength back. I didn't want to go to such a seemingly dark place. But I did want to complete the art practice.

I wept through several meditation periods alone in the Heron Hut. I wept for those who suffer loss from war, oppression, and injustice. I wept for those in my family who died in the Holocaust. I wept for parents who bury their children. I simply needed to cry.

Back in the studio I took up the thickest coil, the five-foot section of the tug-of-war rope. I suspended it, tied it, uncoiled part of it, and wove the strands back into itself. I threaded thin white twine through it, the way a snake coils around a stick. The heavy loop circle of rope looked like a Japanese Enso, the circle that expresses form and emptiness. My sculpture of death hung in front of me, immanent. It was beautiful and simple. The thin white line wove through it, a ray of light.

I was then asked to propose a sculpture for a mill building being developed into condominium units. Still trying to regain my strength, I knew I didn't want to work alone. I asked a friend Margot Stage if she wanted to collaborate.

"Wow," she said in her strong deep voice, upon seeing the string constellations hanging in my studio. Margot's voice was well known to listeners of WGBH, one of Boston's public radio stations. She'd been a producer and host for more than twenty years, and then left radio to pursue her own art-making. We were both delighted to have the opportunity to work on a project together. We ordered more rope, and on our own we each filled three garbage bags with masses of looped string and rope. We met at the farm and began tying all the ropes together, cascading them from a second level porch. We used the thicker ropes at the top and added in smaller diameter threads closer to the bottom. Our sculpture, *Source*, echoed the natural fall of water.

Later, the developer decided against any art, but we exhibited *Source* at the farm's annual outdoor sculpture exhibit, hanging it from a high limb of a pine tree near the pond. Gravity kept the heavy rope in place, but a gentle wind teased the lower twined loops reminding me of the elm tree I had seen when I first visited the farm. *Source's* threads tickled the water, like the elm's graceful branches.

Margot and I decided to continue to work together, and our next project was for The Arsenal for the Arts, an art complex in Watertown, Massachusetts, outside Boston. We created a larger waterfall from rope and twine that cascaded several stories over a central staircase. This installation then traveled to Cape Cod for an exhibition outdoors on the Provincetown dunes. Moving the sculpture from indoors to outdoors, from the human built staircase to the natural dune landscape on the Cape was satisfying. The threads we had knotted together gave a *sense of place*, no matter where we installed it. Art was the healer. The fibers were doing their mending.

The monastery's art practice had given me an opportunity to creatively explore the emotions I had encountered during the time of my treatments: grief, depression, and fear. Collaborating with Margot brought me off my sofa and back into the world. ❧

Row 23: Girdled Trees

In early April, the apple buds began to open, earlier than I had ever seen them. I called Gus to let him know we were ready for his bees. He brought two hives after three days of eighty-degree temperatures. It felt like June, shorts and t-shirt weather. However, the day after the bees arrived, the daytime high dropped to fifty-three, and that night the temperature was in the low forties. The next day I cranked up the wood stove. Putting on a fleece jacket, I walked out to check the bees. Not a one in sight. They hadn't ventured outside their hives since they had arrived. I wondered if they were still alive and began to worry. The forecast was for rain throughout the next week and temperatures well below average.

Email alerts came in from the University of Massachusetts Extension Service announcing freezing temperatures for the next two nights. We might lose the crop. So much work, so much commitment. So much money. The emails suggested setting up water sprayers to coat the buds and keep the air circulating in the orchard. What could I do? We didn't have a windmill to provide air circulation, and we had no irrigation in

Vole-gnawed bark, 2014

the orchard. I couldn't set up sprayers to mist the buds to keep them from freezing. I could get on the tractor and spray water all night long, but the sprayer wasn't hooked up, and I just didn't have it in me. I had never sprayed at night. I wasn't even sure the tractor had headlights. It all seemed hopeless.

I stopped looking at the weather reports. It didn't matter. In the orchard blossoms were at peak bloom. We had three cold, wet days, and then, finally, a beautiful afternoon. Finally, the orchard was filled with the sound of bees. I hoped somehow we would have fruit, but most of the blossoms were plastered on the ground, and the bees were on the ground, too, pollinating the dandelions. I called Gus to pick up his hives.

A week later, I knew for certain we would not have a crop. No apple trees to thin; the orchard was not going to bear any fruit this year.

I visited Frank Carlson again, wondering how his trees had fared. Frank was rested and tanned, recently back from Florida, where he and his wife go for a few months' break from the apple world. Frank told me during the cold snap he'd recorded two nights of thirty-six degree temperatures. But Old Frog Pond Farm's orchard slouches back toward a large wetland where the cold air settles in and stays. The cold had destroyed our blossoms, while his trees on an open hillside did fine.

First a year of cancer treatments and now a year of no apples. Was the world trying to tell me something? What was I doing wrong? Maybe I should just let the orchard go. I had made a go of it, I had learned a lot, and had grown some great crops of organic apples. It was a gallant effort, but I had failed.

July brought no rainfall. New England was in the midst of a severe drought. In fact, in July 2012, over eighty percent of the United States was experiencing drought conditions. I filled and filled the three-hundred gallon spray tank and drove through the orchard to give twenty-five gallons of water to each young tree every week. It took days and lots of diesel fuel, but it saved them. Perhaps it was good we didn't have fruit. The apples would have been small. The trees would have struggled to support a crop without adequate water.

I had missed the holistic apple growers meeting because of my treatments, but I returned on the first Wednesday of March 2013. Michael, Alan, Brian, John, Scott, and Hugh all gave me hugs and welcomed me back. I shared with the group about the frost. Hugh, a biodynamic grower, spoke about valerian, an herb that can be sprayed for frost protection. Known by many for its help with insomnia and keeping depression at bay, valerian, when sprayed right before a freeze, can raise soil temperatures by two degrees. I made a note about it. I would plant a patch so I would have it on hand for the future. This comradery, like the Sangha at the monastery, inspired and supported me. Even without a crop, I was an organic apple grower. I returned home with new ideas. I would not give up.

I filled out an application to the Natural Resources Conservation Services (NRCS), part of the USDA, for a grant to put in an irrigation system, and we were accepted. The trees would surely benefit from irrigation. Blase installed it with a few hired hands. All of the water used to irrigate the farm would be pumped from the surrounding pond and wetlands.

With water, I could plant all kinds of beneficial and medicinal plants in the orchard: plants that are good for our soil, and plants I hoped would help with pest management. I could implement some of the teachings from the Japanese orchardists I admired. Caleb had retired, and we had hired our neighbor, Paige. We planted echinacea, mountain mint, snakeroot, chives, Jerusalem artichokes, borage, valerian that Blase had grown from seed, and more comfrey between the trees. We moved many of the plants from other locations on the farm. The beauty of the orchard delighted us as summer progressed.

By midsummer, I was irrigating twice a week because it was so dry. The water helped the orchard's native wildflowers: milkweed, Queen Anne's lace, St. John's wort, yarrow, red and white clovers, asters, chicory, yellow wood-sorrel, and feverfew. Then I'd hear the pump come to a slow stop. *It's out of fuel*, I thought. *No, it's clogged*. Blase would strip down and wade up to his chest in muck to pull weeds away from the foot valve that draws water into the pump. But it was worth the effort to have irrigation, the orchard was beginning to feel like a natural woodland and the trees were loaded with a bumper crop of fruit after their season of repose.

I started tasting apples in early August. We were growing a new early-season, disease-resistant variety, Pristine. Named for its pristine scab-free skin, it's an apple developed by the disease resistant breeding program PRI—Purdue University, Rutgers, and Illinois University, the same group that offered Williams Pride, the apple John Bunker had grafted onto a row of our Red Delicious trees.

At the end of August, when Blase asked if he should mow in the orchard. I replied, "Not yet, no." The Jerusalem artichoke flowers were six feet tall, colorful beebalm was everywhere, mountain mint, St. John's wort, comfrey leaves, and the valerian stalks swayed with dried flowers. A few weeks later he brought up the subject again, "I'm going to mow the orchard." Again, I said, "No, not yet."

My enthusiasm for the apple bounty was still measured; a brief hailstorm could ruin a crop. I needn't have worried. We had a bumper crop of apples. The weather was perfect every weekend in September, and we had just one rainy day in October. I didn't need to advertise; people came in droves to pick organic apples.

Our rustic kitchen was a festival of canning supplies—jars and lids, funnels, pots, and food. Baskets of peppers, onions, and tomatoes became huge pots of simmering tomato sauce; chopping boards of peppers, zucchini, and tomatoes became ratatouille; and bowls of raspberries and mountains of snowy sugar melted down into sparkling raspberry jam. It was always a surprise to hear the popping sound as each lid sealed. Making jam is labor intensive, but seeing glistening rows of color made it all worthwhile. And we always sold as many jars of jam as we produced.

Heavy snow fell in January 2014. The drifts were more than three feet high, burying the lowest limbs of the trees in the orchard. I had never seen so much snow. In early February, warmer temperatures brought a thaw, melting first around the trunks. My eye caught sight of gnawed wood close to the ground, a glowing bright orange color. Shocked, I reached down and brushed more snow away. The gnawed wood went deeper.

Voles! They had scampered across the crust of the deep snow, climbed over the eighteen-inch-high hardware cloth fence encircling every trunk, and dropped down between the trunk and the protective screen. There they made soft, grassy nests, and ate and lived in the safety of their cozy burrows, with a pantry of their favorite food close by. In tree after tree, these pesky rodents had eaten the bark, chewing their way around the base of the trees and down to the roots. Tree after tree was girdled, the grooves in the bark cutting off the sap flow between the roots and the crown. Girdling, when complete, kills the tree.

I panicked and called in reinforcements. With a couple of friends, we started shoveling the snow away from the trunks. It was exhausting work. How could we remove that much snow from every tree? When we were too tired to shovel, we stomped the snow down with snowshoes. It felt like a war zone. Our hats, coats, shirts, and gloves were scattered everywhere; we had stripped to tank tops, but it was too late. The damage was done.

Paige made a detailed map of the injured trees and numbered them on a scale of one to four. One was one-quarter girdled, two was halfway, three was three-quarters, and four was completely girdled. We decided to cut down the threes and fours, the ones with the worst damage. I couldn't imagine cutting down any more though I knew a weakened tree attracts diseases and pests. We removed fifty trees out of 300. Such quick work to take them down compared to years of cultivating growth. All that time and expense, all the potential fruit. The saw-sharp silence of marked trees was not for the faint of heart.

I didn't want to think about killing off voles, either, but I would have to do something. It had been a bumper year for voles. Nature is like that—a bumper year for acorns, for apples, and now, for voles.

Commercial growers knock down the vole population every fall with pellet poison. I had done the opposite. I had created a perfect vole habitat by growing delicious herbaceous perennials and cultivating long grasses and flowering plants between the trees. Following the irrigation drip lines, the voles had scampered freely from tree to tree. I would have to rethink my approach and mow down the perennials. So much for our wild orchard.

I decided to replant the apple trees we lost, but most commercial nurseries sell out of fruit trees by late fall, and I had a hard time finding trees. Finally, I found a small Amish nursery in New York State that had fifty Crimson Crisps, a tree I already grew and liked, another PRI offering. Its apples are so bright red even before they are ripe it is hard to keep the customers from picking them.

In mid-April the trees arrived and we replanted. The sprayer was clean and ready for our first spray. But this year was different. When I walked through the orchard I didn't see blossoms. Where were the flowers? Only the rows of the Liberty apples had flower buds. I didn't believe what I was seeing, but I had to admit, again, we would not have a crop. Last year had been a bumper crop and now nothing.

It was the same all around; all over New England commercial orchards were already putting in insurance claims, and I was receiving calls from other small Massachusetts apple growers. They had nothing either. It was a mystery. Some people blamed biennial production. Others said the colder than normal winter temperatures had damaged the buds, the native pollinators weren't out, or winter moth damage. No one really knew.

With Paige's help, we beefed up the farm offerings. We had a summer of art classes, a series of Sunday programs, a bluegrass concert, another performance of Walt Whitman, an expanded outdoor sculpture exhibit, and an open studio. Although it was a terrible year for apples, it was a great one for raspberries. With some careful sprays, building up the nutrients in the soil, and by daily removal of any old fruit, we managed to keep the *Spotted Winged Drosophila* at bay. We made batch after batch of jam. Paul Willard, a farmer in Harvard, said, "It's like the old wives' tale. When it's bad for apples, it's great for pumpkins." He had never had such a good pumpkin year.

In November when the season ended, Blase mowed the orchard aisles, and I used a gas-powered weed-whacker to knock down the grasses growing between the trees. Mole and vole trails were everywhere. A pair of red-tail hawks arrived and I was comforted to think they were eating well.

Paige and I made sure each tree had a solid hardware cloth cage and a donut of pea stone around the trunk. With their tender snouts, voles stop when they encounter sand or stone. We couldn't afford to suffer any more rodent damage. ❦

Row 24: Harvest

The winter that followed was good for the orchard. We had normal and consistent cold temperatures. I checked the apple trees in early spring and was relieved to see only a small amount of vole damage. I observed each blossom stage—silver tip, green tip, bud, tight cluster, pink, and blossom.

Our bee-man Gus had finally retired, and Charlotte, a beekeeper from Lincoln, Massachusetts, brought us a hive instead. The apple blossoms looked like a Van Gogh painting, but when I walked through the orchard I didn't hear that wonderful incantation of buzzing bees. I was nervous about pollination. Charlotte was concerned they might have lost their queen in transit so she brought another hive. I saw other insects making their way through the blossoms—bumble bees, ants, and insects I couldn't identify—but only the occasional honeybee.

After petal fall, I was surprised to see the pollinated applets start to plump. Clusters of five and six apples from each blossom filled every branch on every tree. The native pollinators along with the honey-bees had done their job. I attributed our pollination success to all the

Ariel picking Honeycrisp apples, 2017

wildflowers we had encouraged in the orchard and throughout the farm. I even wondered if we would need to bring in honeybees next year. Could I trust the native pollinator population would be enough? Charlotte didn't think so, and I never experimented. Don Rota, a beekeeper, approached me about bringing his hives to live permanently on the farm. He was looking for a healthy home with lots of forage for his bees.

When I asked Don why he loved to keep bees he wrote:

> . . . to watch a colony swarm into the air. And then to be
> able to safely coax this amazing force-of-nature safely
> into a new home. It's quite a visceral feeling to be able
> to employ this old world alchemy. It's as close as one
> comes to catching lightning in a bottle.

By early fall orbs of color hung from leafy branches—green, red, golden, striped, splashed bronze, and blushed yellow. It was thrilling to see, like when a magician conjures a flock of doves out of colorful silk scarves. In the early morning, as I walked down the cart trail along the orchard to the Heron Hut to meditate, the slanting light lit the many hues of the fruit. I had never seen so many apples in the orchard—2015 was another bumper year.

For opening weekend of both the sculpture exhibit and pick-your-own apples, I knew we were going to be shorthanded. We were now showing the work of thirty sculptors in our outdoor exhibit, "Around the Pond and Through the Woods." We had days of preparation still to do. Ariel, was in Florida working at a dressage barn, but I asked if she would come up to help out. We had maps of the exhibit to finish, signage for each piece, and parking to organize. Ariel arrived and got to work, making signs, and finishing the map. She was right on target with everything that needed to be done. The plan was for her father to pick her up late Sunday afternoon; they would have dinner together and then he would drive her to the airport for her return flight.

Sunday was even busier than Saturday, and I was running out to the orchard, back to the farm stand, around the sculpture walk, and back to the orchard. I was surprised when Paul and Ariel appeared in front of me on the cart trail. It was a joyous sight and one that made my heart skip a beat. I never imagined I would see Paul in the orchard. He was a little shy, not demonstrative, but I could see sweetness in his hazel eyes.

"Oh, hi!"

"We're off to the airport," Ariel said.

"I'm so happy you found me," I stammered.

"We wanted to say goodbye," Paul added. And we gave each other a hug.

A month after our orchard meeting, I called Paul. Ariel had been in the professional equestrian world as a barn manager, riding instructor, and high level competitor for over a decade, but it was time for her to try something else. She had devoted herself to this world, missing family holidays and vacations, and much of normal teenage life. I knew from phone conversations she was depressed and she had no idea what she should do or how to make the change.

I called Paul and asked if he'd have lunch to talk about how we could help her. I picked him up in Groton and we went to a local café. We talked about all of the children; our three, his four older ones, and Blase's two children. We talked about our art projects. This was the first time we had shared a meal just the two of us since we had separated sixteen years earlier. When we were through eating, I drove Paul back to the home we had shared for twenty years, the Old Baptist Church with the bell tower, steeple, and the gold weathervane of two geese flying. Before he got out of the car, I said, "Paul, thank you for everything. I am so grateful for our relationship. I will always love you."

Blase had always encouraged me to talk with Paul. He would say, "Your relationship has changed, but you are still in a relationship." In fact, independent of me, Blase cultivated his own relationship with Paul, meeting occasionally for coffee or a meal. Knowing of Paul's propensity for inventions, Blase suggested maybe he would work on a water-driven prayer wheel to replace the old and rusted generator by the dam.

I mentioned this to Paul when we were having lunch, and he didn't answer about the prayer wheel, but said, "You know, Linda, I have a large sculpture I could install."

The Olympic Bell is an interactive sculpture Paul made for an outdoor exhibit at the 2004 Summer Olympics in Athens, Greece. A horizontal, tubular bell is played by pulling a thick rope that lifts a hammer. Its release sends a haunting vibration through the bell, as a low F-sharp resounds. I told Blase, and he agreed it was a wonderful plan. Paul came over and the three of us found the right location, a clearing with one large stump where a tree had come down a few years ago, in the woods but overlooking the pond.

Following the drawings Paul made for the installation, Blase prepared the site. He constructed the wood forms for the concrete base, and found a cement company willing to risk driving on the old cart road to deliver ten yards of concrete. Like the day the sprayer arrived, the incongruity of this massive truck deep in the woods was shocking—but one that was most appreciated. If we had had to mix that much cement by hand it would have been a lot more work.

Paul was away in France at the time of its installation. Blase and a friend went to pick up the bell and loaded it on a flatbed truck with help from Ken, Paul's shop assistant. The parts arrived at the farm and installation began. Ken had experience having put the piece up and down twice before. Blase and Ken worked together using a block-and-tackle to raise the heavy pieces fourteen feet in the air. When the bell first rang, a beaver swam over. The reverberating sound must have traveled through the water and made it curious. The bell sound is deep, resonant, and lasts more than fifteen minutes.

The Olympic Bell is a permanent installation in our annual outdoor sculpture exhibit. Hundreds of people every year enter the grove of tall pines surrounded by wildflowers, walk up to the bell, and ring it. They stand in the quiet listening to its reverberating sound, deeply listening, feeling its satisfying note. I hear in its ringing a tribute to the healing possible between people.

Not long after our lunch together, Paul called me with a question. He was getting his things in order, art and artifacts collected over his lifetime. "Linda, there's one thing I haven't resolved," he said. "I have all your letters. Will you take them?"

"Of course," I said. I already had all of his.

Then he added, "I was about to take one last look at them, but my assistant already put the box in her car."

His assistant arrived. I helped her lift a heavy, locked box out of her trunk. "Thanks, Wendy!" I said.

"You know, Linda, after you left, Paul asked me to order this fire-proof safe. He organized all your letters to him from Japan and stored them safely."

The box was so heavy I asked Blase to carry it upstairs to the room where I have all my Zen books and painting supplies and closed the door. I nervously put the key in the lock. Opening the heavy lid, I lifted out three glasses. Delicate hand-blown sherry glasses we had bought together from Simon Pierce, and on the bottom of each one Paul had etched the date of our marriage. Then I moved my hand across the hundreds of pages of onion skin paper, all the letters, filed by date, letters I had sent Paul from Kyoto during the months after we had met. In the back of the file was a fold-out map. Paul had charted the departure and arrival of every one of our letters, mapping their crisscrossing journey across the globe. I was stunned to see it again after so many years.

Once when Alex and his wife, Connie, were visiting in Massachusetts after a lunch with Paul at the Church, Connie mentioned she had seen the stem from the "apple." Paul had kept the stem I had eaten from that long ago apple on a bus ride in Japan in a tiny jar all these years.

I have only a few physical mementos from two decades together, but I did have three pocketknives. Identical Swiss Army knives that Paul had taken apart, removing the red plastic covering with the Swiss Army insignia, and replacing it with smooth ebony wood like the knife he had used to cut the apple in Japan. Paul had etched "Linda Matisse" on the largest blade on one knife. On the blade of a second knife he had inscribed "Linda Hoffman," and on the third knife he had etched: For Anna, on Christmas, 1985 with love from Paul.

For Christmas 2020, I sent "Anna's knife" to Alex who lives outside Asheville, North Carolina, with Connie and their two daughters. The knife that said "Linda Matisse" I sent to Nick who lives in Juneau, Alaska, with his partner, Kia.

In 2017, Ariel made the difficult decision to leave the horse world and came to live with Blase and me at the farm before finding a room of her own in Cambridge. She started helping me in the office while she looked for a job and we started collaborating on a sculpture for my exhibit "After Apple Pruning" where I used pruned apple branches for all the artwork. It had taken time, but apples eventually infused my art. Ariel did the grafting of the branches using copper wire to create a large tree and I populated it with bronze figures. We titled the piece *Grafting a Life*. After a challenging transition, she transformed her training as a dressage rider into a gifted artist making wire sculptures of figures and trees. The knife that says "Linda Hoffman" I will give to Ariel who lives near me in Watertown with her partner, Ethan.

The graceful elm over the waterfall is no longer alive. Ravaged by Dutch elm disease, we had it cut down. My friend who had first told me to visit the farm came a few days before the tree company. Dressed in black, she sat for several hours, taking leave of the tree. I promised I'd make her a sculpture with some of the wood. A crane and a chipper arrived. Blase was so sad when they pulled up he went inside to weep in private. The tree men started taking it down branch by branch. When Blase came out from the house and saw they intended to put all the wood into the chipper, he told them, "Hey, guys, I want the board wood." He would mill, stack, and dry it, and then, make something with it, a piece of furniture, or some other project.

"No," they said. "It's too much work."

"Then you can leave now," he said. "I want the wood."

The tree removers agreed to put aside the board wood for him. Blase used it to make a beautiful set of elm and walnut cabinets for our kitchen.

If there has been a consistent lesson between the orchard, Zen practice, and my life, it is that nothing is permanent. Last year, a neighbor called and said there is a proposal to change the zoning of a large parcel of land in Boxborough to allow the building of four warehouses totaling a million square feet. The land is located within two thousand feet of our orchard. Blase and I went to Boxborough board meetings, joining many others to protest. With much pressure from local residents, the zoning change was deferred, and the article was pulled from the upcoming Town Warrant. But the fight is far from over. The development company owns the land, and town residents still have to find a way to work with their representatives to create something that will benefit the town and keep the wetlands protected. More development means more runoff, weeds, and pollution, and it could affect our capacity to irrigate the orchard. Though we've had a few years without fruit, we're still on the map for organic pick-your-own apples.

In 2018, after a few good apple seasons, we had almost no crop. An unidentified disease made the leaves brown and dry in late August. It was so bad I didn't even want to walk into the orchard, let alone let anyone else see it. I thought maybe this was the end of growing apples. I didn't know what to do. Something was wrong, the trees were suffering, and I didn't know why.

I learned at the next Holistic Apple meeting it was a new fungus from Asia, Marssonina leaf blotch. Apple leaves become covered with black blotches and then the living tissue dies. It was first identified in Pennsylvania in 2017 and then traveled up the coast. The spore release is similar to scab. Organic growers in Europe are controlling it with their regular scab spray program. Not knowing about it, and not needing to spray for scab in July, I hadn't sprayed. Now I know, even without the worry of scab, I still need to spray fungicides into summer, especially during wet springs. It's not yet time for me to get rid of my sprayer as Hugh, my apple grower friend, suggested at the first Holistic Apple Growers meeting I attended fifteen years ago. ❀

The Last Row

Today I visited the brush pile back of the orchard. Here the trimmings of the winter are placed, waiting to be burned when dry. How many are the archives that will be destroyed! Here are histories in every bud and twig and scar, of the seasons, of the accidents, of the deaths, the records of the tree as there are records of families. These records are not written in numbers or in letters, nor yet in hieroglyphs: yet they are understandable.

—Liberty Hyde Bailey

Grafting a Life, sculpture with Ariel Matisse, 2017

Orchard Mandala

A jeweled hoarfrost covers the ground. Its crystalized needles sparkle in winter's slanting rays. In the orchard every branch on every tree is covered perfectly with a sleeve of ice. The orchard at Old Frog Pond Farm is a living sculpture, a multidimensional mandala to contemplate and cultivate. We have years with good crops, harvests of bumper crops, and seasons with no crop. We host African drumming classes, morning meditation, solstice fires, forest bathing, art exhibits, concerts, poetry readings, memorial services, and weddings.

Blase and I were married in the sacred circle in 2014. Our best friend, Ron, who lived with Blase when we first dated, ministered our vows. We took liberties with the Sufi mystic Hafiz's poem that begins:

> Our union is like this: If you feel cold, I will reach for a blanket to cover our shivering feet.

We added our own verses:

> Blase: If you feel hunger I would run to my garden and start digging potatoes.

Snow on branches

Linda: If you are longing for something sweet,
I will pick raspberries and drop them one by one
onto your tongue.
Blase: If you are ever lonely, I will show you the
face of love is everywhere.
Linda: if you are sad, I will show you amazement
in a field where a thousand spiders' webs connect
every blade of grass . . . .

Moussa Traore, a master African drummer from Mali, drummed a celebratory song when we gathered after the ceremony and planted a beech tree. My stepfather Bill, the oldest person at the wedding, gave the first toast. Bill has remained an ardent supporter for me and my children though my mother died more than twenty years ago.

Blase and I were surprised when several of our children chose to offer their own toasts. Alex, the oldest of our children, offered the first one, then Blase's daughter, Brigid, spoke of how grateful she was to have a model of two people who could support each other in healthy ways and independently follow their own passions. Nick then shared how moved he was by the care Blase provided during my cancer treatments.

My mandala is not created with colored sand, but with each tree, rock, insect, nest, vole, visitor, poem, drumbeat, prayer, plant, poet, bird, meditator, caterpillar, moth, and snake. The mandala never remains the same. Wind gusts blow down a tree, a frost freezes the buds, the bees swarm, a new sculpture arrives. One year there are nettles near my studio, the next year they move closer to the chicken coop. This year milkweed is popping up everywhere, maybe inspired by Alicia Dwyer's sculpture installation, *Continuation Migration*, a long fence painted with hundreds of monarchs to raise awareness of the fragile migrations of these threatened butterflies.

At the Intergovernmental Science-Policy Platform on Biodiversity and Ecosystem Services (IPBES) in Paris, the 2019 report said, "The health of ecosystems on which we and all other species depend is deteriorating more rapidly than ever. We are eroding the very foundations of our economies, livelihoods, food security, health and quality of life worldwide."

Our planet faces a ferocious loss of habitat and biodiversity. We're a destructive species causing the acidifying of the ocean, the loss of precious topsoil, and the poisoning of the very air we breathe. The animals and insects haven't caused this harm—we have. But I like to think, despite our recklessness and selfishness, they would choose to save us. In my bronze sculpture *Refuge*, a young giraffe rides on the back of a sea turtle. Both of these endangered species portage humans on their backs towards safety.

Mystical moments arrive unexpectedly in the brushwork of clouds over the orchard at sunset and in the quaking orange of a pair of orioles among the green leaves of an apple tree. Yet it is living season to season, on this land, tending it year after year, that I see the nurturing and inspiration the farm offers. With each new season we hire a couple of returning farmers and a couple of young ones who are putting their hands in the earth for the first time. We plant greens in the hoop house and vegetables in the field. The perennial crops ripen beginning with asparagus, then rhubarb, mulberries, goumis, blueberries, gojis, peaches, raspberries, and pears. But it is the apples that really define the season. Williams Pride and the yellow Pristine, our earliest apples, then the Honeycrisp and Liberty. The midseason Jonafree, Galarina, Crimson Crisp, and Golden Crisp, and finally the late russets and Denis's favorite apple, the Esopus Spitzenburg.

When Denis asked recently, "What's your favorite apple?" I said, "I don't have a favorite apple. I like eating them all."

He then replied, "Tom Burford, one of my mentors, always answered, 'The next one that is ripe.'"

The winter months are quiet. The farm is covered with a blanket of snow and the pond is indistinguishable from the land. Through the bare branches of the catalpa tree outside my studio, I can see the front rows of the orchard. It's time for winter work—pruning the apple trees. Each pruning cut changes the future growth of the tree. The Buddha said the same thing two thousand five hundred years ago. Every action creates karma: nothing arrives by itself, there is always a causal condition. If we want healthy bodies, we have to grow healthy food. If we want a healthy planet, we have to put healthy inputs into the soil, the water, and the air.

We held off the developers of the giant warehouses on the parcel in Boxborough that abuts the orchard, but now there is a pharmaceutical company planning to move into one of the existing buildings. Townspeople are concerned about their use of biological and hazardous materials. This is new territory for the town: they have no established bio-safety levels for biotech waste. Not only could waste leach into the wetlands that feed our orchard, the leach field is located in an Aquifer Protection area. We'll be attending the upcoming meetings.

Our beekeeper, Don, sent me an email in early March: "Good News!" After a decade of lobbying by beekeepers across the state, a motion was passed unanimously by the Massachusetts Pesticide Board Subcommittee to restrict the use the neonicotinoids. This is good news, but at the federal level, in January 2020, the EPA proposed only "interim decisions" for this class of pesticides. Their plan is to require spraying when the bees are not present, require people using the products to wear more personal protective clothing, along with "language on the label that advises homeowners not to use neonicotinoid products." Clearly they know these insecticides are bad for the environment, bad for insects, and bad for humans, yet a ban similar to many in Europe is not yet in sight. We have to continue putting pressure on our legislators and educating the public. The global Covid pandemic has shown we are interdependent and interconnected. A ban on hazardous pesticides needs to be worldwide. Otherwise, companies will simply move their sales from countries where they are prohibited to countries where they are allowed.

※

Denis arrives on a frosty morning. I carry in my pocket our updated orchard map, 343 trees, 103 varieties of apples listed by row, a map that changes as new trees grow and old ones transform into sculpture, fire-wood, and ash. It's been a year since I've seen him, a full year since we've been in Covid quarantine. I put on my facemask to receive the carton of fresh eggs he has brought. Then we walk into the orchard. We each hold a pair of loppers, our handsaws dangle from our belts. We begin pruning, noticing the fruit buds, the leaf buds, the mystery of new growth.

We start in the rows with the mature Yellow Delicious trees. We study these gnarly, old ones, and make some large pruning cuts.

"This is a beautiful tree," I say.

"Yes!" Denis replies and adds, "I think it is my favorite."

They are friends we have grown to love. Then we smile because we say the same thing when we greet the next tree. I never take the map out of my pocket. I know the names of most trees. And the ones I don't remember, Denis recognizes.

Each tree lives a complete life. Although growing in the same orchard, each tree writes its own narrative, encounters its own challenges. Denis and I do what we can to help. We let one grow tall and slow another's growth. We remove a large branch in the upper part of a tree to encourage growth below. We cut back branches that have grown into the aisles where the tractor needs to drive. We open up windows for the pickers to get to the fruit. Above all, we prune to encourage the fruiting wood, we prune to let in the light. ❦

Old Frog Pond Farm, 2021

Acknowledgments

A large community of artists, poets, seekers, and farmers have contributed to the evolution of Old Frog Pond Farm, and to each one of you, I am grateful!

Over the years it took to complete this book, many people read chapters, drafts, or discussed the book with me. In particular, I want to thank Susan Alexander, Louise Berliner, Martha Bustin, Al DeSetta, Linda Fialkoff, Judith Hertog, Moira Linehan, Susan Richmond, Margot Stage, Judith Schutzman, bg Thurston, Gabrielle White, and Allison K. Williams. To my writing group, Christine Colacino, Lisa Fliegel, and Roxana von Kraus, thank you for unwavering belief in this book.

To John Bemis, John Bunker, Frank Carlson, Michael Phillips, Alan Suprenant, Hugh Williams, and the holistic apple community, I wouldn't be growing apples without you. To Denis Wagner, friend and apple pruner extraordinaire, I hope we will be pruning together for many years ahead.

Sangha, sculpture, 2008

Much gratitude to Kavita Hunt, who found our copper listed on an old OMRI list—and for so much more!

Nine bows to Shugen Roshi, Hojin Sensei, and Hogen Sensei, Zen teachers at Zen Mountain Monastery.

Lynn Horsky, thank you for the work on many projects and now bringing your great creative spirit to the design of this book. Thank you to Paul Marion and Loom Press—a perfect press and editor!

With deep appreciation to my closest family: Bill, my stepfather, my brother, Jon, my children, Alex, Nick, and Ariel, their father, Paul; and my stepchildren, George, Michael, Robin, Sophie, Brigid, and Blase, Jr..

Blase, for your generous heart, endless curiosity, and infinite patience. Old Frog Pond Farm is an expression of our love for each other, our children, the earth, and our community.

My mother, Anna (Dr. Annette Weiner), the pulsing thread throughout the book. In writing this memoir, I hope I have done what you wanted me to do—to share what it means to take risks, to venture off the map, to follow through despite the naysayers.

Elizabeth Ainsley Campbell who sent me to visit the farm when I was looking for a place to live.

The Spauldings who planted the orchard and cared for this land for many years.

The indigenous Nipmuc people who first lived here. I acknowledge this land was your land, and it was stolen from you by the European colonists. I offer a portion of the proceeds from the sale of this book to be donated to the Citizens of the Nipmuc Nation to help preserve and promote the culture of your ancestors for future generations.

And to those people who will become stewards someday, I hope you will continue to offer it as refuge for all sentient beings. ❦

A Note on the Author

An honors graduate of Bryn Mawr College with a degree in Fine Arts, Linda Hoffman studied at the *Sorbonne* and at the *École Internationale de Théâtre Jacques Lecoq* in Paris. Awarded a Thomas J. Watson Fellowship after graduating from college, she trained for two years in the Noh Theater in Kyoto, Japan.

A lifelong passion for poetry converged in 1981 with her work as a graphic artist in the form of her first sculpture, a poem in cloth, launching an extensive exploration of narrative sculpture incorporating language, natural fibers, wood, stone, and found objects. In 1997, she began using old agricultural tools to create lyrical and poignant sculptures decrying New England's vanishing agricultural landscape. Represented in museums and private collections, Hoffman has public sculptures installed in towns and cities across the region.

A contributor to WBUR's *Cognoscenti*, Hoffman was a founding editor of *Wild Apples, a journal of nature, art, and inquiry.* She is the author of three chapbooks of art and poetry and the letterpress art book *Winter Air*, created in memory of her mother, Dr. Annette Weiner.

In 2006, five years after Hoffman and her three children moved into an old farmhouse with an abandoned orchard, Old Frog Pond Farm in Harvard, Massachusetts, became the first organic pick-your-own orchard in Massachusetts. Now, with more than fifteen years of apple experience growing organic apples, Hoffman contributes to a holistic growers' forum, teaches workshops, and is respected by an influential holistic apple growing community.

She lives with her partner, Blase, his parrot, Orco, and friends who move in for a few days, weeks, or a season who are part of the farm's growing creative and spiritual community. A Zen Buddhist, Hoffman's *dharma* name *Shinji* means Truth in the Soil. *The Artist and the Orchard: A Memoir* is her first book. ❦

They can speak, trees,

they can say the sweetest things . . . .

—Hafez

References

Uncultivated: Wild Apples, Real Cider, and the Complicated Art of Making a Living by Andy Brennan

Apples: The Story of the Fruit of Temptation by Frank Browning

Apples of North America: Exceptional Varieties for Gardners, Growers, and Cooks by Tom Buford

Apples and the Art of Detection by John Bunker

The One-Straw Revolution by Masanobu Fukuoka

Old Path White Clouds: Walking in the Footsteps of the Buddha by Thich Nhat Hanh

Akinori Kimura's Miracle Apples by Takuji Ishikawa. Published with an introduction by Yoko Ono on her Imagine Peace website.

Apples of Uncommon Character by Rowan Jacobson

Riding the Ox Home: Stages on the Path of Enlightenment by John Daido Loori

The Apple Tree by Liberty Hyde Bailey

The Holistic Orchard: Growing Tree Fruits and Berries the Biological Way and *The Apple Grower: A Guide for the Organic Orchardist* by Michael Phillips

The Botany of Desire: A Plant's-Eye View of the World by Michael Pollan

Wild Apples: The History of the Apple-Tree by Henry David Thoreau